CIRIA C578 London 2002

Brownfields – managing the development of previously developed land

A client's guide

D W Laidler

A J Bryce

P Wilbourn

CIRIA *sharing knowledge* ■ *building best practice*

6 Storey's Gate, Westminster, London SW1P 3AU
TELEPHONE 020 7222 8891 FAX 020 7222
1708 EMAIL enquiries@ciria.org.uk
WEBSITE www.ciria.org.uk

Brownfields – managing the development of previously developed land. A client's guide

Laidler, D W; Bryce, A J; and Wilbourn, P

Construction Industry Research and Information Association

CRIA C578   © CIRIA 2002   RP633   ISBN 0 86017 578 2

Keywords

Contaminated land, environmental good practice, ground improvement, ground investigation and characterisation, housing, land use planning, pollution prevention, procurement, project management, regulation, risk and value management, site management, sustainable construction, sustainable resource use

Reader interest	Classification	
Land-owner, developer, contaminated land officer, planning officer, environmental and engineering consultants, investor	AVAILABILITY	Unrestricted
	CONTENT	Guidance document
	STATUS	Committee-guided
	USER	Landowners, developers, clients, local authorities

Published by CIRIA, 6 Storey's Gate, Westminster, London SW1P 3AU.

British Library Cataloguing in Publication Data

A catalogue record for this book is available from the British Library.

Summary

The UK Government's expressed policy of utilising previously developed land provides a golden opportunity for developers to profit by developing such land, provided that they and their professional team have the requisite skills to capitalise on this precious land resource.

With a target for 60 per cent of new houses to be accommodated on such previously developed sites, developers need to acquire the necessary know-how to manage such sites or they will be left behind in the move towards a more sustainable approach to land resources in the UK.

This guide, however, is directed to more than just housing on previously developed land. Many of the same issues face clients engaged in commercial, industrial and retail sector developments. Some businesses have already carried out significant amounts of successful development on such land and have the advantage of being ahead of their rivals, but others have been put off by what they perceive as unacceptable risks and uncertainties with these sites.

Recent research has identified some specific issues that often arise when these sites are being developed. While they may be unfamiliar to some in the development industry, they can be managed in much the same way as other development risks and opportunities.

This guide provides a framework for managing these issues logically and methodically. The issues are addressed using the normal stages of the development process, so that the client can readily incorporate the guidance into his own management systems.

The guide can also help the client identify his own technical limitations and identify where such outside assistance is needed. It equips the client with the tools he needs when appointing and managing a specialist team of advisers to monitor them successfully.

The overall aim is to instil confidence in those presently lacking the knowledge to handle such projects and assist clients in acquiring the skills necessary to handle what will become the mainstream of property development in the UK.

The guide has been prepared following extensive consultation with those involved in land development and reflects much of the best practice guidance employed in the UK to which CIRIA has already made a substantial contribution.

Acknowledgements

Research contractor	Parkman Ltd		Andrew Bryce and Co	Wilbourn Associates
Steering group chairman	Ms V Fogleman			
Funders	Department of Trade and Industry (Partners in Innovation Programme)	NHBC		The Royal Bank of Scotland
	Cleanaway	Scottish Enterprise Lanarkshire		TLT Solicitors
	English Partnerships	Shell Global Solutions		Welsh Development Agency (WDA)

This is the project report for CIRIA Research Project 633: "A client's guide to building on brownfield sites". It is one of a series of guidance documents and case studies on remedial treatment of contaminated land. The purpose of this research is to encourage good practice and improve the confidence of construction professionals when building on previously developed land.

Parkman Ltd, in association with Andrew Bryce and Co and Wilbourn Associates, undertook the research under contract to CIRIA. The principal authors of the report were Douglas Laidler, Andrew Bryce of Andrew Bryce and Co, and Philip Wilbourn of Wilbourn Associates. Photographs are courtesy of Parkman Ltd and Lattice Property Holdings.

CIRIA wishes to express its thanks to the members of the project steering group for their contributions to the work:

Ms V Fogleman (chair)	Barlow Lyde and Gilbert
Dr P Beckwith	British Waterways
Mr P Braithwaite	Ove Arup and Partners International
Mr E Cooke	TLT Solicitors
Mr P Crowcroft	Environment Agency (now with Entec)
Mr K Deady	ASDA Stores Ltd, part of the Wal*mart Group
Mr G De Roy	Tyser (UK) Limited
Mr G Duckworth	Environment Agency
Mr M Dyer	Cleanaway
Mr M Fearnley	Halcrow Group Ltd
Mr P Fisher	Scottish Enterprise Lanarkshire
Mr C Gooderham	Andersen
Mr D Graham	Royal Bank of Scotland
Mr B Guillaume	Ove Arup and Partners
Dr T Henman	Enviros Aspinwall
Dr G Lethbridge	Shell Global Solutions

Mr E Poole	English Partnerships
Mr S Smith	Welsh Development Agency
Prof P Syms	Sheffield Hallam University
Mr J Wilson	WS Atkins
Mr S Wood	Lattice Group

CIRIA's research manager for this project was Ms J C T Kwan.

Funders

CIRIA and the authors gratefully acknowledge the support of the following funding organisations:

Department of Trade and Industry (Partners in Innovation Programme)

Cleanaway

English Partnerships

NHBC

Scottish Enterprise Lanarkshire

Shell Global Solutions

The Royal Bank of Scotland

TLT Solicitors

Welsh Development Agency (WDA).

Case study materials

CIRIA would also like to thank the following individuals who provided case study materials during the research:

Dr P Beckwith	British Waterways
Mr K Deady	ASDA
Mr G de Roy	Tyser (UK) Ltd
Mr J Harrison	British Waterways
Dr T Henman	Enviros Aspinwall
Mr P Hughes	Birse Construction Ltd
Mr T Jenkinson	Tony Jenkinson Tax Consultants
Dr S Johnson	CERTA (UK) Ltd
Mr S Smith	WDA
Mr M Tilt	British Waterways
Mr N Trollope	Fairview Homes

Contents

LIST OF FIGURES

LIST OF TABLES

Glossary

Conceptual model A textual or graphical representation of the relationship(s) between contaminant source(s), pathway(s) and receptor(s) developed on the basis of hazard identification, and refined during subsequent phases of assessment.

Contaminant See **Source**.

Contaminated land (for the purposes of Part IIA of the Environmental Protection Act 1990) Any land that appears to the local authority in whose area it is situated to be in such a condition, by reason of substances in, on or under the land, that:
a) significant harm is being caused, or there is a significant possibility of such harm being caused or
b) pollution of controlled waters is being, or is likely to be, caused.

Contaminated site Any site that, as a result of activities either previously or currently carried out on it, contains concentrations of substances or pathogens high enough to be a hazard to health or the environment either in the current use of the site or if it is used for a different purpose (Royal Commission on Environmental Pollution, 1996, *Sustainable use of soil*, 19th report).

Controlled waters All fresh and saline natural waters up to the UK offshore territorial limit, including rivers, streams, lochs, estuaries, coastal waters and groundwater. The statutory definition of controlled waters is given in the Water Resources Act 1991, s 104(1) and the Control of Pollution Act 1974, s 30A(d).

Derelict land Land so damaged by industrial or other development that it is incapable of beneficial use without treatment.

Desk study Interpretation of historical, archival and current information to establish where previous activities of the land were located, and where areas or zones containing distinct and different types of soil contamination can be expected to occur, and to understand the environmental setting of the site in terms of pathways and receptors.

Detailed investigation Main on-site investigation involving sampling and analysis to characterise ground conditions for a specified purpose; may be undertaken as a single stage or as several successive stages.

Exploratory investigation Preliminary limited intrusive investigation/analytical work of a site, to provide preliminary information on the condition of the land.

Flora and fauna Plants and animals including livestock (agricultural and game species), crops and plants used for landscape and amenity.

Greenfield site An area previously undeveloped and therefore undisturbed with a predominantly consistent subsurface.

Harm Adverse effects on the health of living organisms or other interference with the ecological systems of which they form a part. In the case of humans the definition includes harm to property.

Hazard A property (of a substance) or situation with the potential to do harm.

Hazard assessment A conceptual stage of risk assessment concerned with assessing the degree of hazard associated with a particular site or group of sites.

Hazard identification	An initial conceptual stage of risk assessment concerned with identifying and characterising the hazards that may be associated with a particular site or group of sites.
Made ground	Material artificially in place comprising a wide range of materials, such as concrete, tarmacadam, brick materials.
Pathway	The means by which a hazardous substance or agent comes into contact with a receptor.
Planning Policy Guidance notes (PPGs)	Documents embodying government guidance on general and specific aspects of planning policy to be taken into account in formulating development plan policies and in making planning decisions.
Pollutant linkage	The relationship between a contaminant (source), a pathway and a receptor.
Potentially contaminated land sites	Sites identified (while undertaking desk studies/site investigations) as being, or having been, subject to a land use that may give rise to contamination
RAMSAR site	Wetland of international importance, especially as a waterfowl habitat. Designated under the Ramsar Convention on Wetlands of Importance 1971 (Ramsar Convention), which places general and special obligations on contracting parties relating to the conservation of wetlands throughout their territory.
Receptor	The entity (for example, humans, animals, water, vegetation, buildings) that is vulnerable to the adverse effects of a hazardous substance or agent.
Redevelopment	New construction or conversion, usually by the private sector but often with public-sector support or participation, of previously developed land and/or buildings.
Remedial action	Action taken to mitigate or reduce defined unacceptable risks. Remedial treatment and remedial works are specific examples of remedial action.
Remedial options	Options for mitigating or reducing defined unacceptable risks.
Remediation (of contaminated land)	A form of risk management that ensures the land is suitable for use.
Risk	The probability that an adverse effect will occur under defined conditions.
Risk assessment	The process of assessing the hazards and risks associated with a particular site or group of sites.
Risk estimation	A conceptual stage of risk assessment, concerned with estimating the likelihood that an adverse effect will result from exposure (of the receptor) to the hazardous substance or agent.
Risk evaluation	A conceptual stage of risk assessment (generally following risk estimation) concerned with evaluating the acceptability of estimated risks, taking into account:

- the nature and scale of risk estimates
- any uncertainties associated with the assessment
- the broad costs and benefits of taking action to mitigate the risks.

Risk management	The process whereby decisions are made to accept a known or assessed risk and/or the implementation of action to reduce the consequences or probabilities of occurrence.

Risk management objective	A statement of what must be achieved in order to mitigate unacceptable risks.
Source	A hazardous substance or agent that is capable of causing harm. For pollutant linkages, the source is termed a contaminant.
Special Site	A site where the contamination is such that the Environment Agency has become the enforcing authority for the purposes of Part IIA of the Environmental Protection Act 1990.
Stakeholder	Any individual, group or organisation that may affect, or be affected by, or perceive itself to be affected by, risk.
Statutory consultee	National public organisations/bodies that need to be consulted on planning applications, depending on the nature of the development and its location.
Supplementary investigation	Investigation, carried out subsequent to a detailed investigation for the purpose of refining risk estimation, to assist in the selection of an appropriate remedial strategy, or for detailed (remedial) design purposes.
Vacant land	Land that was previously developed and is now vacant that could be developed without treatment.
Warranty	An express or implied statement forming part of a contract that a particular state of affairs exists.

ABBREVIATIONS

Abbreviations used in this guide are listed below.

AGS	Association of Geotechnical and Geoenvironmental Specialists
BBA	British Bankers Association
BDA	British Drillers Association
BGS	British Geological Survey
BRE	Building Research Establishment
BSI	British Standards Institution
BURA	British Urban Regeneration Association
CBI	Confederation of British Industry
CDM	Construction (Design and Management)
CES	chartered environmental surveyor
CIA	Chemical Industries Association
CIC	Construction Industry Council
CIRIA	Construction Industry Research and Information Association
CIWEM	Chartered Institution of Water and Environmental Management
CLAIRE	Contaminated Land Applications in the Real Environment
COSHH	Control of Substances Hazardous to Health
CPA	comprehensive project appraisal
cpo	compulsory purchase order
DEFRA	Department for the Environment, Food and Rural Affairs
DETR	Department of the Environment, Transport and the Regions
DoE	Department of the Environment
DTI	Department for Trade and Industry
DTLR	Department for Transport, Local Government and the Regions

EA	Environment Agency
EU	European Union
FOE	Friends of the Earth
FSA	Financial Services Authority
HA	Highways Agency
HBF	House Builders Federation
HMSO	Her Majesty's Stationery Office
HSE	Health and Safety Executive
ICE	Institution of Civil Engineers
IChemE	Institution of Chemical Engineers
IEHO	Institute of Environmental Health Officers
IEMA	Institute of Environmental Management and Assessment
IP	Institute of Petroleum
ISO	International Standards Organisation
LPC	Loss Prevention Council
LQS	land quality statement
MAFF	Ministry of Agriculture Fisheries and Food
MNR	marine nature reserve
NAMAS	National Measurement Accreditation Service – see **UKAS**
NFHA	National Federation of Housing Associations
NHBC	National House Builders Council
NNR	national nature reserve
NPPG	National Planning Policy Guidance
NRA	National Rivers Authority (now Environment Agency)
NRPB	National Radiological Protection Board
PIA	Pensions Investment Authority
POST	Parliamentary Office of Science and Technology
PPC	Pollution Prevention and Control
PPG	Planning Policy Guidance
PPG(**)	Pollution Prevention Guidance notes – SEPA/Environment Agency
RICS	Royal Institution of Chartered Surveyors
RPG	Regional Policy Guidance
RTPI	Royal Town Planning Institute
SAC	special area of conservation
SEPA	Scottish Environment Protection Agency
SiLC	specialist in land condition
SNIFFER	Scotland and Northern Ireland Forum for Environmental Research
SPA	special protection area
SSSIs	sites of special scientific interest
TRL	Transport Research Laboratory
UKAS	United Kingdom Accreditation Service
UKELA	United Kingdom Environmental Law Association
UTF	Urban Task Force
WDA	Welsh Development Agency
WRc	Water Research Centre

TARGET READERSHIP FOR THE GUIDE

The *Client's guide* is aimed at clients who take decisions on development projects and/or who manage the process. The guide's readership will consist of:

- house-builders and other developers
- landowners
- local authorities – as landowners and developers
- speculative developers
- owner-occupiers
- public-sector landowners, other than local authorities
- funding partners.

Property professionals, including lawyers, surveyors, consultants, contractors and regulators, will also find the guide helpful.

Because the guide identifies issues and interactions within the overall process, local planning authority professionals should also find the document a useful reference.

HOW TO USE THIS GUIDE

This book is intended as an initial reference for clients involved with previously developed land. The accompanying wall-chart acts as an introduction and a prompt to help entry into the guide itself.

In its role as a route map, the guide incorporates summaries of the key issues of relevance to the development process. Table 1.1 in Chapter 1 provides an overall schedule of these topics and where they may be found in the guide. A list of the topics dealt with at particular stages of the development process is included at the start of each chapter. The guide also includes cross-references (shown as [xx]) to more detailed guidance.

Lists of the main documents relating to the various stages of the development process are included at the end of each chapter. These incorporate good practice and policy documents published by policy-makers, regulators, and research, trade and standards-setting bodies.

Chapter 1: Opportunities for brownfield development

This provides an initial entry point into the guide focusing on the opportunities available in developing previously developed land. The chapter includes an illustrative graphic of the various chapters that comprise the *Client's guide* together with the summary list of topic headings (Table 1.1). This allows readers to dip in and out of the guide.

Chapter 2. Previously developed land – issues and interactions

Chapter 2 considers the definition of previously developed land, key interactions and related wider guidance on redevelopment.

Chapter 3. Preparing for development

This chapter reviews factors considered to be important by those involved with previously developed land. It provides guidance on devising a development strategy, covering the setting of objectives, establishing one's own limits of expertise and structuring a project team. Chapter 3 also contains summary information on who may be involved in the consultation and approval process and emphasises the importance of managing information.

Chapters 4 to 8. Stages in the development process

These chapters broadly reflect the development process, starting with site acquisition and planning, running through design and construction, and concluding with site management or disposal.

The guide recognises that land development is rarely, if ever, a sequential process and stages often overlap or run in a different sequence. For example, the guide envisages detailed investigation being undertaken immediately prior to the detailed design stages. Circumstances may well dictate, however, that this aspect is required as part of site acquisition. In this way, the guide will help clients identify issues within a familiar framework.

Abbreviations/Glossary/References

These sections are included to assist readers to find further information should they require it.

Appendices

Thirteen appendices provide more detail on various issues covered in the main body of the document. These include references to relevant Scottish, Welsh and Northern Ireland guidance.

The guide's structure provides clients with a route map set within a familiar framework. It brings together those financial, legal and technical issues that are likely to be key factors in decision-making in the development of previously developed land or buildings.

It will also enable these issues and associated action points to be addressed in relation to recognisable milestones and so be readily incorporated into clients' project business plans. The guide is aimed principally at clients who may be new to such projects, but it should also provide some prompts for clients more experienced with previously developed land.

All clients, from the more experienced to those with little or no experience in dealing with previously developed land, need a range of skills to organise their project teams. These skills may come either from the client's own capabilities or from professional advisers. This guide helps clients identify any resources they may be missing and gives support on the selection of advisers.

The guide aims to facilitate timely assessment and forward planning of projects, and thereby to reduce the potential for:

- missing opportunities
- experiencing potential pitfalls.

By providing a framework of a client's management plan, the guide supports these objectives by facilitating initial pre-planning and offering a continuing management tool that may be used to track the issues and outcomes as a project develops.

RELATIONSHIP OF THIS GUIDE TO GUIDANCE AVAILABLE FROM CIRIA AND ELSEWHERE

A considerable amount of new guidance has been, or is being, produced as a result of recent legislation and government policy initiatives on environmental protection and land regeneration.

In the context of contaminated land, for example, policy-makers and regulators have issued the technical tools that enable landowners (and their advisers) to identify problems and then tackle them effectively. Behind these front-line initiatives is a wealth of sectoral and best practice guidance developed by professional bodies, research groups and associations, and trade and professional bodies.

Appendix 10 lists various bodies that have been involved in producing such documents relating to previously developed land.

As a leading research association, CIRIA is a notable and respected contributor whose substantial portfolio of good practice guidance documents cover contaminated land management, sustainable development issues, geotechnical engineering, environmental management and protection, and health and safety.

Although summaries are provided to describe the issues, this guide does not attempt to detail this existing guidance. Instead, key guidance from authoritative bodies is referenced at the end of each chapter, which acts as a starting-point from where the detailed material (and further extensive referencing) may be accessed.

Chapter 1

Opportunities for previously developed land

Chapter 1 introduces this *Client's guide* and provides an overview of the structure. It also summarises the opportunities presented by previously developed land, which are described in detail within the body of the guide. The chapter includes a signpost summary of where these and guidance on other issues are covered in later chapters to help users be selective in the aspects they may wish to consider.

In conclusion, the chapter shows how the guide may be used as a bridge between clients and their advisers.

1.1   INTRODUCTION

Figure 1.1   *Finished housing development from a previously used site*

Within the UK pressure to use land for development can be intense. Previously used land may be either vacant or derelict. There is also a substantial amount of empty or under-used commercial property with potential for conversion.

Appropriate use of Britain's limited land resources, particularly the reuse of previously developed land, is central to the UK Government's objective of ensuring sustainable development, as described in DETR [1].

In response to pressures being placed on greenfield sites, the government has declared in DETR [1] its aspirations for 60 per cent of new houses to be accommodated on previously developed land and within building conversions. In its publication *Household growth* [2], the government projected that 4.4 million new households are likely to be formed in England by 2016. The debate on where and how homes are to be accommodated has focused attention on previously developed land and the opportunities and risks associated with it.

This guide is not just directed to housing on previously developed land. Clients engaged in commercial and industrial development face many of the same issues. Many such clients, whether they are in the public or private sector, have recognised that opportunities will indeed flow within both the housing and commercial sectors when building on previously developed land. Other clients, however, may not have embraced this area of redevelopment for a variety of reasons.

The guide aims to improve confidence in developing the appropriate team and to provide pointers on the key issues and how they can be handled in order to derive the benefit of opportunities and to manage the risks.

This chapter considers the opportunities that may be available from previously developed land and concludes by providing signposts to the subsequent chapters that clients will recognise as a broad route map of the development process.

1.2   STRUCTURE OF THIS GUIDE

Figure 1.2 illustrates how the chapters of the guide relate to the development process.

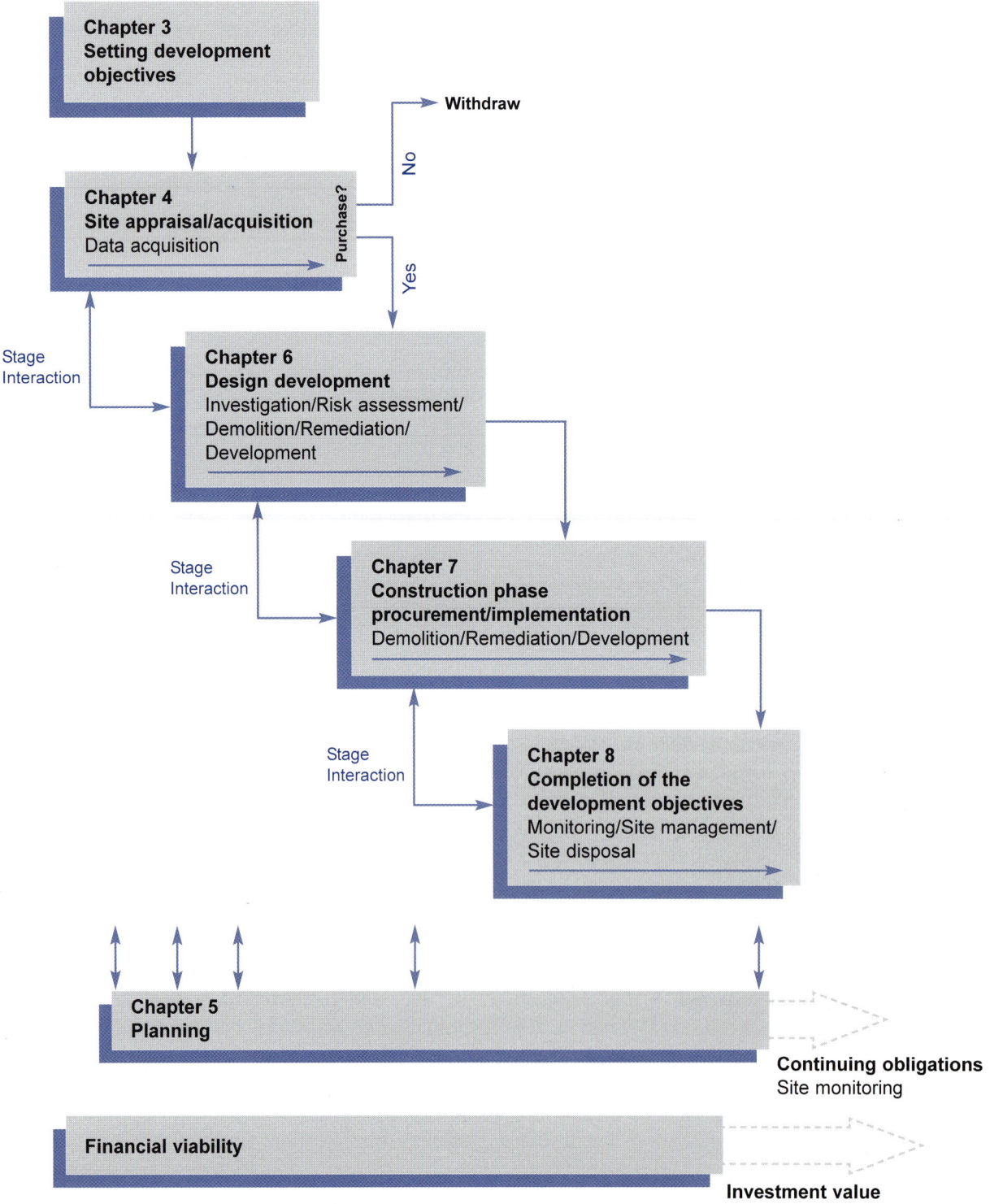

Figure 1.2   *Stages of development – interactions and overlaps*

Chapters 4, 6, 7 and 8 describe particular stages of development that should be familiar to clients. Chapter 5 covers planning issues that often interact with all stages. Each chapter covers issues relevant to the stage in question and places them in context within the development process.

In practice, development is not a linear process where one stage is completed before the next is started. With previously developed sites in particular there will often be significant overlaps and interaction of activities between the various stages. This guide is not, therefore, a project blueprint. Rather, it is a route map to help clients identify the key opportunities and issues and where they may occur within the development process.

With the guide structured in readily recognisable stages, it is envisaged clients should be able to integrate issues within their existing management systems.

1.3 OPPORTUNITIES PROVIDED BY PREVIOUSLY DEVELOPED LAND

Sound management and control of the factors that can be experienced with previously developed land will do much to optimise the viability of such schemes. This guide will help clients develop a management framework and improve their awareness of the key issues. In addition, specific opportunities may be available to improve a scheme's viability and thereby to promote a project. These are summarised below, with pointers to sources of further background information within the guide.

1.3.1 Partnership support for regeneration

Partnership support for land and property regeneration schemes may be available from development agencies.

Case Study

Public-private joint initiative
Major waterfront development

A major port's landholder owned some 79 hectares of under-used or derelict land in a local town. Due to port operational, tenancy and infrastructure constraints, the best means of reclaiming the land to bring it back into active use was a joint initiative between the development agency and the landholder. As a component of the initiative, each party would make agreed inputs, with the returns from land disposals being shared according to the ratio of those inputs.

The reclamation works have removed a massive visual blight from the area and have dealt with large areas of land contaminated with asbestos, hydrocarbons and heavy metals. Rationalisation and relocation of intrusive and "bad neighbour" uses has meant that such businesses have re-grouped alongside other industries away from the town. This, together with the provision of new infrastructure, has released land for residential, retail, commercial and leisure development. In financial terms, it appears likely that both parties may fully recoup their input investments, demonstrating the success of the joint initiative.

Lessons learned

To make this joint initiative work it was essential:

- that the initial site assessment, treatment strategy, development proposals and development appraisal were robust and conservative
- the development agency's broader economic regeneration aspirations for the local town were balanced with the necessarily more focused commercial aspirations of the port's landholder for its landholdings and port operations
- the confidence of the local community was raised and support obtained for what might have been seen as yet another doomed "artist's impression" for the docks
- the legal agreement had to both bind and protect the interests of both parties while enabling decisions, spending commitments and directional changes to be made quickly and compliantly.

1.3.2 Identifying tax advantages

Potential opportunities in respect of previously developed sites include:

- ***tax incentives for contaminated land***

The May 2001 Finance Act included a provision for companies to claim tax relief on 150 per cent of the remediation expenditure on developing contaminated land. Appendix 8 gives illustrative case study details.

- ***VAT***

VAT on qualifying expenditure may be beneficial. The situation should be carefully evaluated when deciding whether or not to elect for VAT for a project, particularly if it is a refurbishment project.

- ***landfill tax exemptions***

Exemption from landfill tax may be an important consideration within the overall financial appraisal of previously developed land.

- ***stamp duty***

From 30 November 2001, in the UK's most disadvantaged areas certain property sales, assignments of existing leases and grants of new leases will be exempt from *ad valorem* stamp duty. Chapter 4 gives details.

Further information

1 **Tax incentives**. See Chapter 4, *First steps – site appraisal and acquisition*.

2 **VAT**. See Chapter 4, *First steps – site appraisal and acquisition*.

3 **Landfill tax exemptions**. See:
   Chapter 4, *First steps – site appraisal and acquisition*
   Chapter 6, *Design phase*
   Chapter 7, *Construction phase*.

4 **Stamp duty**. See Chapter 4, *First steps – site appraisal and acquisition*.

1.3.3   Exploiting sustainable development criteria

Increasingly, the principles of sustainability are being applied to the justification of a scheme, its design and construction, and the continuing management of the final scheme. This is relevant to the redevelopment of previously developed land and, indeed, to all developments.

Chapter 2 includes a brief introduction to the RICS/Environment Agency guidance, *Comprehensive project appraisal* [3], and its proposed framework for assessing project sustainability (CPA) in the context of evaluating planning applications for schemes in the light of sustainability criteria. Redevelopment of previously developed land provides particular opportunities for contributing positively to the sustainability of a project in comparison with using a greenfield site. This can, in turn, contribute to driving proposed schemes forward. Potential benefits that can be derived from schemes on previously developed land are shown below:

- the redevelopment of brownfield sites in preference to greenfield sites
- the reuse of contaminated land
- improving land by remediation
- improving quality of surface waters/groundwaters
- reuse and recycling of materials
- conservation/biodiversity – maintaining sensitivity to the contributions from existing land condition

- interaction with existing industry types – contributing to the diversity of industry and overall industrial development
- existing landscape – enhancing its nature and beauty
- heritage – harmony with local heritage, and buildings and sites of historic significance.

> **Further information**
>
> 1   See Chapter 6, *Design phase – potential range of issues through the design stages of demolition, remediation and development.*
> 2   See Chapter 7, *Construction phase – regarding issues at design stage being carried over to construction.*

1.3.4   Opportunity-led development

Redevelopment of sites and properties on previously developed land becomes opportunity-led when sites are available and situated in the right area to meet economic and business objectives and when the appropriate exit strategy is in place.

The balance between supply-driven and opportunity-led development is considered further in Appendix 1.

1.4   SIGNPOSTS TO ISSUES IN THIS GUIDE

For users of this guide who may wish to be selective, Table 1.1 provides a schedule of the issues and topics contained within the various chapters and appendices. Those chapters and appendices dealing with topic areas in rather more depth are shown in **bold**.

Table 1.1   *Information sources within the guide*

Topic area	Chapters	Appendices
Advisers – selection, appointment and review of capability	3 4 6 7	A3 A10
Advisers – adviser's management plans		A6
Archaeology	4 6	
As-built information	8	
Brownfields – government policy		A1
Clients – management plans	3	A5
Communications	6	
Conceptual model	4 6	
Consents/permits/licences	4 6 7 8	A7
Consultations	6	
Contact addresses – policy-makers/regulators		A10
Contact addresses – research organisations/professional bodies		A10
Contamination – on previously developed sites	2	A2
Contamination – existing land use	2	A2
Contamination – new land use	2	A2
Contractors – prequalification, selection and engagement	4 7	A4

Continued on next 2 pages

Topic area	Chapters	Appendices
Data management	3 4 5 6 7 8	A11
Design – implementation	7	
Development community – factors of importance	3	A1
Development of sites – integration with remediation	6 7	
Dovetailing guidance – *Model procedures for managing contaminated land*	2	
Dovetailing guidance – *Comprehensive project appraisal*	2	
Environmental assessments – requirements	5	
Environmental protection	4 6 7 8	
Exit strategy	3	
Financial – satisfying provisions for mobile plant licences		A9
Financial review	8	
Financial risk	2 3	
Funding strategies	4	
Health and safety	4 6 7 8	
Indemnities	8	
Insurance	7 8	A9
Investigation – strategies	4	
Land condition records (LCRs)	3 8	A11
Land quality statements (LQSs)	3 6	A11
Landfill tax exemptions	6 7	
Leasehold transactions	8	
Legal issues	4	A13
Marketing/publicity	8	
Monitoring	6	
Nature conservation	6 7	
Northern Ireland – policy		A12
Opportunities for land development	1	A1
Part IIA		A2
Parties to the process – planning/building control/others	3	A10
Partnership support for regeneration	1 4	A8
Planning – conditions	5 7 8	
Planning – consultees	5 6	
Planning – developing the team	5	
Planning – policy appraisal	5	
Planning – applications	5	
Planning – and site investigation	5	

Topic area	Chapters	Appendices
Planning – information needs	5	
Planning – emerging guidance	5	
Planning – negotiations	5	
Planning – scope of applications	5 8	
Previously developed land – definition	2	A1
Project management	3 7	A3
Protected species	5	
Redevelopment – design guidance	2	
Regeneration agencies		A10
Remediation – integration with development	6 7	
Remediation – strategy and design	6	
Reporting – schedules of reports	4 6 7 8	A11
Risk management	3 4 7 8	A1 A9
Site acquisition – options and strategy	3	
Site assembly/site ownership	4	
Site log	3 4 6 7 8	A11
Site verification – strategies	7	
Scotland – policy		A12
Solicitor's warning card		A13
Stamp duty	4	
Strategy development	3	
Suitable for use – the UK Government's approach	2	
Sustainable development issues/criteria	1 4 6	
Tax incentives for contaminated land	4 6 7	
Tax relief		A8
Technical good practice	4 6 7	
Transactions – leaseholds	8	
VAT	4	
Vendors' information	4	
Verification	7	
Wales – policy		A12
Warranties	3 8	
Waste management – disposal and licensing	4 6 7	
Waste management – satisfying financial provisions		A9
Water pollution	7	
Water Resources Act		A2
Websites – policy-makers/regulators		A10
Websites – research organisations/professional bodies etc		A10

1.5 HOW THE GUIDE CAN ACT AS A BRIDGE BETWEEN CLIENTS AND ADVISERS

The guidance is intended mainly for clients who may be new to projects on previously developed land. It covers the key issues and so enables clients to take a view on where and how advisory support may be obtained to create a sound project team. Clients should therefore be able to identify:

- aspects that can be dealt with without assistance
- aspects that require additional support
- the ways in which they can obtain such support.

Clients with greater experience of previously developed land will also find the guide of use, as it will help them identify areas that they may not have considered and alert them to those situations where professional advice is needed to supplement and enhance an existing project team.

The guide, then, acts as a reference document for clients at all levels of experience of previously developed land.

By offering a reference point of this kind for clients, the guide should also be useful for advisers as a framework that sets out the range of needs and requirements of prospective and existing clients. In this way it can form a bridge between clients and advisers and help take forward good practice.

- ### *the client's viewpoint*

The fact that their advisers are (or can be made) aware of the guide as a client support tool should be reassuring to clients. They can take projects forward in the understanding that their advisers know they have access to background information on the relevant issues and on the actions and good practice approaches that may be appropriate.

- ### *the professional adviser's viewpoint*

On the one hand, the professional adviser can use the guide to identify key issues and to communicate his credentials to address them successfully; on the other, he will know that clients will retain access to this support facility. The adviser may recognise that a proactive approach is expected of him. This may include not only communicating their forward plans but also confirming that they retain competence to act on new or changing issues as the project progresses.

The exchanging of viewpoints and approaches by clients and advisers (together with interaction with stakeholders in general) provides an important focus for the guide. As a result, it can also act as a complementary management tool to support value engineering and value management processes that may be adopted by clients to their development schemes.

As a complementary and parallel initiative to this *Client's guide*, the Construction Industry Council (CIC) [37] has published a short briefing guide, aimed at clients who have gaps in their knowledge and experience of developing previously developed land. The *Briefing guide* alerts readers to some of the ways of addressing these gaps and to the standards of intercommunication and approach they should expect from their construction advisers.

Previously developed land – issues and interactions

Chapter 2 looks at what is understood by "previously developed land" and its association with the commonly used term "brownfield land", and considers why such land has emerged as a key component of the government's strategy for land development.

Although it will not be present on every previously developed site, contamination remains an important issue. This chapter also provides a summary of particular guidance documents that are likely to play a crucial in the handling of such sites and shows where this guide will dovetail with them.

Appendix A1: *Brownfield sites – policy and commercial drivers* provides a wider perspective of the pushes, pulls, drivers and interactions that may be involved.

2.1   WHAT IS PREVIOUSLY DEVELOPED LAND?

The term "brownfield land" has been widely used as the general reference for land that has been previously developed in recent years. Other terms, such as "derelict land", "vacant land" and "redevelopment" have also been used. For practitioners, defining what constitutes a brownfield site has been a matter for debate, involving such issues as [4]:

■   whether such a site also has to be a contaminated site

■   whether other common terms that are in use, such as "derelict land" and "vacant land" that may be used in specific but similar contexts, should be accommodated within a definition of "brownfield land".

While "brownfield" helps us visualise the type of land in question, debates on its precise definition are likely to continue. Within this Client's Guide the issues relate to "previously developed land", which is defined in Planning Policy Guidance note PPG 3 *Housing* [1] as:

> *that which is or was occupied by permanent structure (excluding agricultural or forestry) and associated fixed surface infrastructure. The definition covers curtilage of the development (see below). Previously developed land may occur both in built-up and rural settings. The definition includes defence buildings and land used for mineral extraction and waste disposal where provision for restoration has not been made through development control procedures.*
>
> *The definition excludes lands and buildings that are currently in use for agricultural or forestry purposes, and land in built-up areas which has not been developed previously (e.g. parks, recreation grounds, allotments – even though these areas may contain certain urban features such as paths, pavilions and other buildings). Also excluded is land that was previously developed but where the remains of any structure or activity have blended into the landscape in the process of time (to the extent that it can be reasonably be considered as part of the natural surroundings), and where there is a clear reason that could outweigh the reuse of the site – such as its contribution to nature conservation – or it has subsequently been put to an amenity use and cannot be regarded as requiring redevelopment.*
>
> (PPG 3 (2000): Annex C, p 27) [1]

Work on buildings may form part or all of the development activity on previously developed sites. Activities that relate to building conversions and renovations will therefore be relevant to this Client's Guide.

2.2 CONTAMINATED LAND AND PREVIOUSLY DEVELOPED SITES

2.2.1 Introduction

Previously developed land can become affected by contamination through a variety of mechanisms. These include:

- leakage during storage and transport of materials, particularly from underground pipes and tanks
- accidents such as spills
- airborne emissions from industrial processes, eg chimney stacks
- release of harmful substances from development, if not properly controlled
- inappropriate waste management practices.

Many industries have, or previously had, the potential to cause contamination. Not all sites used by particular industries are affected by contamination, and even where they are, not all are affected to the same degree. Sites occupied by similar uses will not necessarily contain the same contaminants or similar concentrations of contaminants; many sites may also have been remediated previously. Sites may also be further affected by contamination problems arising from adjacent land, such as those occurring through airborne emissions or leaching through groundwater. Gas can also migrate through ground or through trenches for services on sites.

Potentially harmful substances occur naturally and this fact should be taken into account when assessing previously developed land. The levels of metals and other elements vary considerably between different soil types. Some rock types can release radon gas, which can reach the surface through fractures and can accumulate in enclosed spaces. Methane gas can also be a natural contaminant, which can be released by coal mining or produced by soil microbes acting on natural organic material in the soil, especially in marshy areas. Methane can accumulate in confined spaces, reaching potentially explosive concentrations.

Previously developed land need not be either contaminated or suspected of being contaminated. Despite this, such land is often construed as inevitably contaminated. Recent research by Syms [4] has confirmed that establishing whether or not a site is contaminated (or, by inference, is in a location likely to be exposed to contamination) remains one of the major decision-making issues within the process of building on previously developed land.

Valuing contaminated land or land that is perceived to be contaminated is difficult for developers and valuers, and they are likely to adjust the yield or factor in the cost to correct the problems. Stigma, which may have an impact on value, may also be an important constraint on many developments.

Development uncertainties as a whole undermine the process of redevelopment and regeneration. They can affect not only development on previously developed land but also opportunities on greenfield sites. Uncertainties can affect developers' abilities to plan their project development strategies fully and this can in turn undermine their ability to obtain finance, for example, or to ensure that the project is successfully let or sold at the end of the construction phase.

The Urban Task Force [5] looked at the issue of contaminated land as a barrier to development. It highlighted the report prepared by the University of Ulster funded by the RICS *Accessing private finance: the availability and effectiveness of private finance in urban regeneration*' [6], which found that 58 per cent of investors saw remediation of contamination as a major negative factor in making their investment decisions.

Among their further findings were:

- there is an institutional view that regards land contamination as a difficult liability. This, in turn, depresses land values and thus reduces the economic viability of regeneration projects
- confidence is lacking in the outcomes of the remediation processes, fuelled by a lack of consistency in the quality of advice provided about the risks involved, and the way in which the advice is presented.

2.2.2 Suitable for use – the government's overall approach to contamination

Where contamination creates risks through the existing use of land, there is now a statutory regime – Part IIA of the Environmental Protection Act (EPA) 1990 [7]. This was inserted into the EPA by Section 57 of the Environment Act 1995 [8] and came into force on 1 April 2000 in England. It was implemented in Scotland and Wales in July 2000 and July 2001 respectively. To date, provisions for Northern Ireland have not been implemented.

This regime deals with risks that relate to the existing use of land and therefore does not cover all situations where contamination is present and may need to be addressed.

The government's wider approach to contaminated land is embraced in a "suitable for use" approach described in DETR's (now DEFRA's) Circular (02/2000) [9]. This seeks to ensure that land:

- is suitable for its current (existing) use
- is made suitable for any new use.

The government views this approach as *the best means of reconciling the various environmental, social and economic needs*". The government has three objectives relating to contaminated land:

- to identify and remove unacceptable risks to human health and the environment
- to seek to bring damaged land back into beneficial use
- to seek to ensure that the cost burdens faced by individuals, companies and society are proportionate, manageable and economically sustainable.

Current (existing) land uses

The Part IIA regime provides a statutory definition of land that is contaminated. This definition is devised for application to the Part IIA regime and relates to the specific duties of local authorities to regulate land within their areas in the context of its existing use.

For England, the secretary of state has used powers under the Act to issue statutory guidance to be read in conjunction with the Act that, among other things, provides a detailed framework for the definition of contaminated land. Separate statutory guidance provisions have been made for Scotland and Wales – see Appendix 12.

The definition is based upon the principles of risk assessment. The statutory guidance follows established risk assessment approaches and involves identifying whether the interaction between a contaminant and a receptor via a pathway is established. This is referred to as the source-pathway-receptor linkage, sometimes also called the contaminant-pathway-receptor or the source-pathway-target linkage. Where such a linkage is identified, this is known as a pollutant linkage; where this linkage is of a form that leads to land being identified as contaminated land in the context of Part IIA, the linkage is termed a significant pollutant linkage.

A substantial body of technical guidance has been and is being produced by such bodies as the Department for Environment, Food and Rural Affairs (DEFRA – formerly DETR), and regulators on its behalf, eg the Environment Agency and the Scottish Environment Protection Agency (SEPA). The guidance provides good practice guidance tools to investigate and identify the nature and characteristics of sources of contaminants, pathways and receptors, thereby providing the means of establishing whether contaminated land is present. These bodies have also developed related good practice guidance directed, for example, at methods by which soil contamination or pollution of controlled waters can be addressed.

Many other organisations, of which CIRIA is one, have also developed guidance covering investigation, assessment, evaluation and management of contaminated land, providing a range of acknowledged good practice.

Further background on the implementation of the Part IIA regime is given in Appendix 2. Contact points for these publishers of good practice are listed in Appendix 10.

Land contamination (or the possibility of it) is a material planning consideration where land is being developed for a different use. Application of the source-pathway-receptor concept in conjunction with good practice guidance is as relevant to redevelopment projects as it is to existing use under Part IIA.

The principles and authoritative advice contained in the good practice guidance used with Part IIA can again be employed as a basis for managing land contamination in the development context, this time taking into account the future use of the land. This framework for applying good practice principles in either regime should give confidence that a consistent approach can be taken both to circumstances on existing land and to proposed new land uses.

For example, clients involved with redevelopment may consider it important to establish whether and to what extent a site remediated as a condition of the planning regime may remain exposed to future regulatory action under Part IIA in what would be its then existing land use.

DTLR and the Environment Agency are developing guidance on responses to planning applications relating to land contamination. This is in the context of the relationships between planning and the Part IIA regime in DTLR [10].

Further information

Further information on Part IIA and how it is implemented is provided in Appendix 2.

Chapter 5 considers planning and in particular the impact of contamination.

2.2.3 Contamination and the impact on financial risk

The impact of land contamination on the financial management of land has been the subject of a major CIRIA research report, *Land contamination – management of financial risk* [12], which examines the relationship between financial risk and land contamination. The report identifies that financial risk stems from:

> *an inability, or perceived inability, to forecast the impact of contamination on business costs, income flow and asset value.*

It concludes that combinations of regulatory, financial and economic and technical and scientific uncertainties contribute to perceived difficulties and a key criterion for developers is the need to formulate their development strategies. This would not only help developers identify available opportunities and maximise the benefits, but also provide a basis for devising forward planning, including strategies for withdrawing from the development cycle, should developers elect to do so.

Management of financial risks from land contamination is considered further in Chapter 3.

2.3 KEY DOCUMENTS THAT DOVETAIL WITH THIS GUIDE

This guide lists examples of the policy documents and good practice guidance that may be consulted at the end of the chapters. A further list of referenced texts is also included before the appendices.

Two documents that are likely to be of particular importance in complementing this guide are described below.

2.3.1 RICS/Environment Agency: *Comprehensive project appraisal – towards sustainability*

Comprehensive project appraisal – towards sustainability (CPA) [3] was published in 2001. It provides a practical framework approach to examining and taking account of sustainability issues, whether a project is on a greenfield site, a redevelopment of previously developed land, or a land management scheme. It is based on the premise that a project appraisal should examine:

- the financial value of a scheme to the developer and the local community as a whole
- the wider economic, environmental and social costs and benefits to arise from the scheme
- variations in views and values held by those who may be affected by the development
- the overall contribution of the scheme to sustainable development.

The CPA document provides a framework allowing evaluation of those project features considered to contribute to sustainable development; it also enables them to be compared with similar evaluations of other development options. Six categories are described in the CPA.

1   Economy.
2   Aesthetics.
3   Natural resources.
4   Public welfare.
5   Infrastructure.
6   Design.

These act as main headings under which features considered to be relevant to project sustainability are listed. For example, two such features, listed under the category "Natural resources" and highlighted in Chapter 1, are likely to have particular relevance to the redevelopment of previously developed land:

- "redevelopment of 'brownfield' sites in preference to greenfield sites"
- "reuse of contaminated land".

Many of the features in the CPA that may have a positive impact on the appraisal process have already been summarised as opportunities for redevelopment in Chapter 1. These will be expanded in the relevant chapters covering the development process.

2.3.2   DEFRA/Environment Agency: *Model procedures for the management of contaminated land*

The DEFRA/Environment Agency's *Model procedures* documents [13] [14] [15] [16] are key technical reference texts in good practice approaches to managing land contamination. These reports are in draft and comprise a hierarchy of interrelated documents that are to be published on a rolling basis.

> The *Model procedures* should offer a benchmark of the good practice approaches for technical advisers. In this respect, clients may not necessarily be technically equipped to handle the various techniques and recommendations.
>
> Nevertheless, they should enable clients to establish how familiar their specialist technical advisers are with the content of the *Model procedures* and to what extent the advisers can demonstrate the way they apply appropriate good practice guidance to the services they are providing.

2.4   DESIGN GUIDANCE ON REDEVELOPMENT

Meeting the challenge of sustainable development has prompted the publication of several complementary development guidance documents covering policy and design principles. Influential guides to assist clients in development design, published in 2000, include:

- DETR's Urban White Paper, *Our towns and cities; the future – delivering an urban renaissance* [17]
- DETR's *By design – urban design in the planning system: towards better practice* [18]
- DETR's *Building a better quality of life – a strategy for more sustainable construction* [19]
- English Partnerships' and the Housing Corporation's *Urban design compendium* [20].

Preparing for redevelopment – setting objectives

This chapter covers initial preparation for redevelopment of previously developed land. It aims to enable clients to give early consideration to the structure and content of their development strategy for a potential site. The chapter provides an overview of the key financial, legal and technical headline issues that may impinge on clients' business planning.

A framework for setting out a development strategy is described that can be developed as a project progresses and act as a practical management tool when used in conjunction with the prompts included in this *Client's guide*.

One of the key principles is that of establishing when and to what extent clients need professional advice to supplement their project team. This is covered in the strategy.

The chapter summarises the potential contacts who may be involved in consultations and the approval process for projects on previously developed land. The importance of effective and robust data management is also emphasised.

3.1 INITIAL PLANNING – FACTORS IMPORTANT TO THE DEVELOPMENT COMMUNITY

Individuals representing a wide cross-section of the land development community have recently offered views on key factors and their relative importance in redeveloping brownfield land, in Syms [4]. Table 3.1 summarises the ranking order of 20 of the most important factors, assigned to five categories that were designated in this research.

Land contamination is prominent within these rankings, comprising six of the top ten factors; these are included within one or other of the research categories:

- site remediation
- site assembly.

Within this guide, managing the implications of land contamination is a recurring issue.

Table 3.1 Key factors of relevance to the development community

Rank	Factor	Funding	Project viability	Site remediation	Site assembly	Regulatory/ policy
1	Financial viability of development	X				
2	Clear advice on remediation methods			X		
3	Land "value"/aspirations of owners	X				
4	Expert advice from environmental consultants			X		
5	Institutional acceptability of investment	X				
6	Ground and surface water contamination			X		
7	Information on previous remediation			X		
8	Geotechnical information				X	
9	Understanding of issues by planners etc					X
10	Soil remediation/treatment costs			X		
11	Risk perception of end-users		X			
12	Data on historical land uses				X	
13	Site location relative to proposed use		X			
14	Quality of site access and local environment		X			
15	Project managers with brownfield experience		X			
16	Set standards for site remediation			X		
17	Quality of documentation			X		
18	Planning constraints					X
19	Capacity of existing services etc		X			
20	Easier land assembly: use of compulsory purchase order powers				X	

3.2 DEVISING A DEVELOPMENT STRATEGY

3.2.1 Supporting the business case

A sound approach to business planning helps clients gain a clear vision of their objectives. By creating an effective framework, clients should also be able to:

- appraise the financial viability of the scheme
- identify and exploit available opportunities
- identify and manage risks
- recognise interactions with third parties
- devise their strategy to withdraw from the development cycle, should it be required.

Creating the clear business case for the scheme will not only contribute to the client's level of confidence, but also assist other parties who may be trying to ascertain whether the site is a sound investment. Additionally, regulators involved in the approval processes may also find it easier to interact with clients when a clear and transparent strategy is in place.

This guide aims to facilitate timely assessment and forward planning by providing the framework for a client's management plan to reduce the potential for clients to:

- miss opportunities
- experience potential pitfalls.

This management plan should also offer the basis for initial pre-planning as well as a continuing management tool to track the issues and outcomes as the project develops.

A key aspect is to help clients establish where gaps exist in their knowledge and capability and where specialist advisers may be required to support the project team. Used in conjunction with the guide, the management plan incorporates prompts for clients to review resources; the guide then offers further assistance on selection of competent advisers.

Case Study

Managing planning – preplanning for development
Creating a developer's manual

With a national land-bank of previously developed sites, a major UK housing developer resolved that the overall management of such sites would benefit from a corporate brownfield handbook.

Using their existing management procedures as the baseline, the management team engaged consultants experienced in development of previously developed land. Working together, the project team developed a working handbook comprising procedures, checklists and sign-off forms for both initial and detailed site acquisition appraisals and also the resulting day-to-day management of their development projects.

Lessons learned

By creating a management framework, senior managers had confidence that commitment to and project management of such schemes is not only consistent but rigorous.

3.2.2 The client's management plan for previously developed land

The client's management plan comprises a framework where clients may:

- scope out the issues and key criteria that will apply to their development strategy
- use the framework as a project-specific management tool to monitor the issues as the project progresses.

Recommended headings are set out in Table 3.2 below. The major components are considered in the following sections, with further details included in Appendix 3. Clients who already have devised management structures should find that the headings can be readily incorporated into their current processes.

Table 3.2 *Framework for the client's management plan*

Headings	Issues
Development strategy	Client's objectives (including financial appraisals)
Potential opportunities	Possible opportunities contributing to the project viability
Screening criteria	Predefined circumstances that, if encountered, could halt interest in a scheme
Acquisition strategy	Specific approaches to acquiring the site in question
Managing risks	Objectives/options to counter financial legal and technical risks, eg insurance options
	Exit strategy – measures to enable a withdrawal, if needed, from the development cycle
Advisers	Gaps in knowledge to be covered by advisers
	Identifying and engaging competent advisers
Contractors	Identifying and engaging competent contractors
Project organisation ■ team structure	Client's internal provisions for ensuring effective project management and supervision are in place The project team is defined: ■ composition and structure ■ specific terms of engagement
Project organisation ■ consultations	Range of statutory and other consultations
Project organisation ■ implementation	Programme and administrative aspects
Project organisation ■ data management	Records to satisfy those (regulators and other parties) who may have interest in the site

3.2.3 Client's site acquisition strategies

The legal options available for acquisition of the land will drive many issues in the early stages of a transaction. Clients will have to consider whether the land should be acquired by:

■ taking an option

■ entering into a conditional contract

■ purchasing unconditionally

■ joint ventures.

The choice may be driven by risk or market opportunism. Considerations may include:

■ planning

■ requirements for site remediation

■ tax

■ funding/grant matters.

The transactional structure will be settled after specialist legal advice has been obtained and may be driven by the level of vendor expectation. Although some previously developed sites may be purchased on a speculative basis, acquisition of potentially contaminated sites and those that require planning permission are likely to be undertaken on a conditional basis or by option. The form of legal documentation may well be driven by risk allocation. See risk transfer and related legal issues in Chapter 4.

Examples of facilitating release of previously developed land in property transactions

Conditional contracts. A major landholder entered into a conditional contract for disposal of previously developed land to a residential developer on a scheme adjacent to a proposed bypass. The contract was subject to:

- granting of planning consent
- the construction of the bypass by the county council.

Obligations included:

- entering into a tripartite agreement involving the county council, landholder and developer to contribute towards construction of the bypass
- a contemporaneous s106 agreement with the city council to abate noise nuisance from adjacent industrial premises at the developer's cost
- requirements for the developer to clean up the site and remove large oil storage tanks, with the landholder obliged to offset the costs to the developer against the "clean site" value.

Option to purchase land. A prospective landholder completed an option to purchase a property. The option cost was negotiated as a proportion of the purchase price. The option was open for a period of 12 months, with an option to renew for a further 12-month period. Upon exercise of the option the sum to be paid would therefore be the purchase price less the cost of the option payments. Should the prospective landholder walk away and not exercise the option, the cost of the option payments would be lost.

Utilising "lockout" agreements and obligations relative to the site. A site was on the market and an offer was made conditional to gaining planning consent and a satisfactory site investigation. A price for the site was agreed and a short form lockout agreement entered into, which prevented the vendor negotiating with any other party over a specified time, eg six months. The purchaser was also obliged to undertake specific tasks relative to the conditional items. Had the contract been breached by the vendor, compensation of the costs incurred by the prospective purchaser would have be payable by the vendor.

Lessons learned

Conditional contracts. Flexibility in constructing conditional contracts provides solutions to releasing previously developed land.

Options to purchase. Options are seen as useful when working with some level of uncertainty with regard to planning consents, contamination or pending a wider site assembly.

Lockouts. Use of lockouts can afford the purchaser security in respect of their costs. This simple form of agreement can often be completed prior to the grant of a conditional contract.

Avoiding significant expenditure until the contractual position has been secured is likely to be attractive. Accordingly, where specialist advice is required to characterise the site, prospective site purchasers may devise specific engagement arrangements with their professional advisers before incurring more substantial professional fees. This is considered further in Chapter 3.

In certain situations, particularly those involving complex sites, costs may be shared. Alternatively, the ultimate price paid may be subject to a formula or specific deductions for investigation and infrastructure costs, giving a development cost and price. Solicitors or clients skilled in property development will be familiar with such concepts for handling unknown costs.

Decision-making at site acquisition
Developing a client report

To aid the evaluation of a potential development, residential developers devised a client report as a reference and collection point for data and opinion obtained from its various specialist departments as an aid to decision-making on acquisition of previously developed sites.

Topic headings included: geotechnical matters, site contamination, site access, services, health and safety, "buildability" of the scheme and exposure to potential liabilities.

Lessons learned

A formalised reporting structure covering key issues provides the client with a reference document for progress to site acquisition.

3.2.4 Managing risks

As with all developments, the objective of developing a previously developed site, whether for residential or commercial purposes, either speculatively or for owner occupation, is to profit from the endeavours. In terms of financial risks, the objective is to set and protect the defined financial objectives for the process.

▶ **exit strategy**

The exit strategy is an integral part of the pre-development planning phase, because the financing or disposal of the assets may be an important way to release the equity and pay off the debt. It enables funds to be recycled into further schemes. In the case of owner-occupiers, this may mean occupying the property at an agreed budgetary level that may not be currently available. Factors covering risk management on previously developed land are considered below.

▶ **managing financial risks**

Clients should consider early planning of this component as part of their overall management strategy.

CIRIA's guide *Land contamination – management of financial risk* [12] notes that where land contamination is involved, uncertainty in the level of financial risk (rather than the risk itself) has been the cause of much of the anxiety in the UK. The type of risk and levels of impairment depend on, among other factors, economic conditions (influencing supply and demand) and the actual and perceived consequences of contamination. Legal liabilities, cost of remediation and any restrictions on the ultimate use of the asset are examples.

This CIRIA guide [12] considered the effectiveness of traditional approaches to financial risk management in the context of legal developments, changes in insurance, accounting and general business practices. These include:

- technical solutions to reduce risks, eg due diligence, remediation
- contractual provisions to apportion liability, eg warranties and indemnities
- traditional insurance to finance loses, eg public liability and property policies.

This CIRIA report covers financial management techniques covering retained risk financing and insurance mechanisms and provides guidance covering the key legal issues, specific risks and options that can be associated with:

- the provision of and reliance on professional advice
- land transactions (mergers, purchases, sales and leases)
- financing and investment
- developing and contracting
- land ownership and occupancy.

▶ *managing legal risks*

Clients need to consider at this stage the level of risk they are prepared to accept in acquiring and developing sites. They need to be prepared to communicate this to their appointed advisers so that risk is appropriately allocated within the contract documents. This is dealt with in more detail in risk transfer in Chapter 4.

▶ *managing technical risks*

Section 3.1 highlighted the importance the development community place on technical issues in the decision-making process. These aspects and the issues to be considered are dealt with throughout the guide.

▶ *insurance*

Use of insurance as a means of managing risks is considered further in Chapter 8. Its role needs to be taken into account in the initial stages of the project to allow for appropriate strategic planning.

3.2.5 Selecting advisers

To clients who are unfamiliar with previously developed land, the range of potential issues can appear daunting. A body of development experience is now in place showing that with the right team, projects can be handled effectively and profitably.

In common with any type of development project, advisers will be engaged to supplement the skills of the project team. They may also be engaged because:

- the consequences of mistakes may be considered too great
- client's resources may be otherwise committed.

Recommendations in setting criteria for the selection of professional advisers are described in Appendix 3. A particular driver that can be critical with projects of this nature is the provision of an effective project management structure to drive the project.

A further issue that can also be critical with such projects is the willingness of the various advisers to agree to provide warranties to underpin advice and activities. This is highlighted in Chapter 8.

For certain sites, a wide range of highly specialist disciplinary skills may be required and many advisers may not be resourced to provide the complete complement of skills. Many sites do not require the full range, either because of the conditions and setting of the site or because high-level guidance is available as a specialist support tool. However, it is incumbent upon all property professionals to be able to recognise situations where either their specific skills and experience are insufficient to the issues relevant to the development or such guidance is not relevant.

In such situations access to additional external advisory support is likely to be required.

> Clients should establish with their prospective advisers the measures they would take to review their professional competence, and the provisions they have in place to consult additional expertise, should the need arise.

3.2.6 Adviser's management plans

As the counterpart to the client's management plan, advisers should be asked to submit an adviser's management plan to help establish the client-adviser dialogue. Topics should include:

- adviser's perspectives of the brief
- planned project responsibilities
- adviser's overall approach to the project
- plans for when and where good practice guidance is to be utilised.

Appendix 5 provides details of the recommended content of the adviser's management plan. As with the client's management plan, the framework should enable initial proposals to be set out and then be monitored as the project progresses.

For those advisers who already have accredited quality assurance procedures in place, their current approaches to projects may well embrace many of the recommended components of such a management plan, so the specific headings should be capable of being readily incorporated.

3.3   WHO DOES WHAT? KEY PARTIES TO THE PROCESS

The roles of the principal players involved in administering and acting as consultees on the regulatory regimes that apply to previously developed land are considered in the Environment Agency's *Guidance on housing on land affected by contamination* [21] and set out below.

3.3.1   Policy and regulation

DEFRA has the principal policy role in environmental protection and a regulatory role in nature conservation and for environmental appeals. In England, DTLR is the appeal body for planning and is a regulator for areas such as consent for harbour works.

In Wales, the National Assembly for Wales is the relevant appeals body. In Scotland, the Scottish Executive acts as the appeals body. In Northern Ireland, application is made to the local division of the Planning Service (part of DOE NI), which consults with the local authority. If the local authority does not agree with the decision, it can ask for the management team of the Planning Service to review it. The applicant has a right of appeal to the Planning Appeals Commission, which is a separate body.

3.3.2   The planning process

In considering development proposals, planning authorities are obliged to ensure that all material planning considerations are addressed satisfactorily. County councils deal with planning applications relating to minerals and waste management. Planning authorities must consult with statutory consultees and may also consult with other organisations and take into account their comments. For example, planning officers take advice on contamination issues from the relevant environmental agency, the local environmental health officer, the Health and Safety Executive (HSE) and building control officers.

A key issue that clients need to address in formulating applications is whether an environmental assessment will be needed. This is considered in more detail in Section 5.4.2.

The principal consultees who may be asked to comment on applications relating to previously developed sites are as follows.

▶   *environmental agencies*

In England and Wales, the Environment Agency is a statutory consultee under the planning process on issues for which it has regulatory responsibility. The Environment Agency advises planning authorities on applications where pollution of surface water or groundwater is involved, or where the water environment might be at risk of pollution as a result of the development. It also advises on applications proposing development close to or on landfill sites and within floodplain areas.

In Scotland, the Scottish Environment Protection Agency (SEPA) is responsible for functions equivalent to those of the Environment Agency in England and Wales. SEPA, however, does not manage flood defence matters.

In Northern Ireland, the Department of the Environment Northern Ireland is responsible for most of the environmental regulation, including the protection of surface and groundwaters.

► *local authority environmental health*

Local authority environmental health departments are primarily responsible for the identification of "contaminated land" under Part IIA. They provide advice to their planning departments on technical matters relating to contaminated land.

These include the discharge of planning conditions, liaison with the environment agencies and certain issues of health and safety both on and off site in conjunction with the HSE (see below). They are responsible for ensuring that certain activities within their jurisdiction do not give rise to a "statutory nuisance." With implementation of the Part IIA regime, the statutory nuisance provisions no longer apply to land "in a contaminated state".

In response to this new regime, local authorities have undertaken steps to handle its implementation, and this department is often the key contact. Other local authorities have made other arrangements for the management of the process and it is advisable to ascertain as early as possible the appropriate contact point.

► *Health and Safety Executive (HSE)*

The HSE is responsible for enforcement of the Health and Safety at Work etc Act 1974 [22] and associated regulations, designed to protect the safety of workers in the workplace or others who may be at risk of harm as a result of workplace activities. This includes the Construction (Design and Management) Regulations 1994 [23].

3.3.3 Building and development control

Building regulations ensure, among other matters, the health and safety of people in and around buildings by providing functional requirements for building design and construction. There are two types of building control providers.

► *local building control*

Local authority building control may be involved throughout construction in enforcing the building regulations.

► *NHBC*

The National House-Building Council (NHBC) is a standards-setting and independent regulatory body for the UK house-building industry. NHBC is also designated as an approved inspector and is able to grant approval under the Building Regulations throughout England and Wales.

3.3.4 Other key parties and their roles

► *environmental agencies – waste management*

The environmental agencies have direct regulatory authority for waste management activities. They issue and maintain registers of waste management licences and certificates of exemption, enforce conditions of licensing and determine whether licences can be surrendered.

The environmental agencies have an oversight role in dealing with contaminated land under Part IIA and are themselves primarily responsible for the regulation of sites designated as special sites. Chapter 7 deals with matters relating to waste management licensing.

► *environmental agencies – controlled waters*

The Environment Agency in England and Wales regulates discharges to and abstractions from controlled waters, as defined in the Water Resources Act 1991, be they surface waters, groundwaters or controlled waters. In Scotland, these are dealt with by SEPA.

► *English Heritage, the Welsh Historic Monuments Executive Agency (Cadw), Historic Scotland and, in Northern Ireland, the Environment and Heritage Service – historic buildings*

These bodies have specific interest in the impact of activities on designated historic buildings and monuments.

► ***English Nature, Scottish Natural Heritage, Countryside Council for Wales – designated sites/protected species***

English Nature is charged with promoting the conservation of England's wildlife and natural features, managing various designated ecological, geological and geomorphological sites as well as protected species. Sites with which they may be concerned include:

- national nature reserves – NNRs
- marine nature reserves – MNRs
- local nature reserves – LNRs
- sites of special scientific interest – SSSIs
- wetlands of international importance – Ramsar sites
- special protection areas – SPAs
- special areas of conservation – SACs.

English Nature advises government on nature conservation issues and acts as a consultee for planning in relation to designated sites. Their consent is also required for carrying out operations relating to SSSIs. Other bodies, including voluntary conservation groups, exist in certain areas.

► ***development agencies***

The roles of English Partnerships, Welsh Development Agency, Scottish Enterprise and the regional development agencies in England are summarised in Appendix 10, which lists contact addresses.

► ***HM Customs and Excise***

Apart from its various revenue-collecting powers, it is responsible for the collection and administration of landfill tax and for the granting of exemptions, in particular that relating to the disposal of historically contaminated land and buildings. See Chapter 7 for details.

► ***utilities***

Situations may arise on previously developed sites where the utilities require the use of specific materials or protection measures as a prerequisite for the installation of services and contact should be made to establish requirements, if any.

► ***water plcs – effluent discharges – sewerage undertakers***

Certain schemes may involve the need to discharge water from the site to sewer, both during and after construction. Establishing whether and on what basis permits can be obtained will be an important element of consultations.

► ***non-governmental organisations (NGOs)***

As with any development scheme, NGOs may have significant impact on progress. With previously developed sites, they may provide active support as well as resistance. Many of these bodies hold useful information in their own right, and clients and advisers can often use the consultation process as an opportunity to obtain background data. This may relate to the site in question, as well as to other sites in the locality. Examples of NGOs are:

- Council for the Protection of Rural England
- Friends of the Earth
- Greenpeace
- Civic Trust
- local interest and community groups.

3.4 DATA MANAGEMENT

3.4.1 Overview – the site log

The efficient management and collation of information is an essential element of successful projects on previously developed sites. Well-organised and readily available documentation about the development can save significant time and expense. As an example of the emphasis on the need for provision of data, the Law Society's *Warning card on contaminated land* [28] highlights the critical need for careful presentation of the facts when a transaction is taking place for any purpose, particularly where contamination is concerned.

It is, therefore, essential that clients create a "site log" as a working file containing site information and records for the site and its development. This acts as both an information source and part of the audit trail required for an ultimate site disposal or letting. The site log should also contain a repository of information relevant to other client obligations, eg requirements under Construction (Design and Management) Regulations (CDM) for information provision to designers and production of the site health and safety file. The creation of a site log should facilitate the collation of these other documents.

▶   *key points*.

When the project starts, clients should bear in mind the following:

▪   *documentation*
   Create a site log as soon as a site is identified.

▪   *location and access*
   The site log should be administered centrally and incorporate systems both to control distribution of documents and copies and to limit access to confidential material. The main system should be centrally based, either within the client's own offices or on site, if adequate facilities exist for this. If on-site facilities are limited, then it is preferable to have a central system with all master documents, and a site-based system with copies. Operation needs to be carefully controlled to avoid the loss of original documents.

▪   *consistency*
   Ensure all relevant managers have written directions for provision of relevant information and documents.

▪   *updating*
   Ensure regular and methodical updating.

▪   *maintenance*
   Maintain the system until a site is sold and do not ignore its maintenance once a site is developed.

> Appendix 11 provides examples of the range of documents to be developed and collated.

Action points

→   Create a site log as soon as a site is identified.
→   Establish administration of the site log.
→   Ensure the site log is updated regularly and methodically.
→   Ensure the site log is appropriately maintained.

3.4.2 Format of records for data collection and dissemination

Various formats for information and record-keeping have been included in published good practice guidance. Those with access to these guidance documents can base the ordering of data on them. Two initiatives have been directed at providing information for third parties, summarised below.

▶ **Land condition records (LCRs)**

The benefits to be gained in greater consistency in handling information on land contamination issues were identified in the Urban Task Force's report in 2000 [5]. The report stated that the benefits of greater consistency in handling information would be:

> to ensure that during the sale, purchase and redevelopment of land, all parties had access to the same data sets and could therefore develop some general agreement between them on the levels of risk associated on that particular site on that particular use.

A working group formed from the Urban Task Force devised a standardised form of land condition record (LCR) [24] for such a purpose, which was launched in November 2000. Its key features are that it:

▨ contains factual information

▨ is completed on the basis of the information available

▨ may summarise information derived from more detailed reports

▨ provides the provenance of any information it contains or to which it refers

▨ uses checklists, standard formats for information and other guidance on its completion as a component of quality assurance

▨ includes information of particular reference to brownfield (ie previously developed) sites and may therefore need to be supplemented by other reports.

The LCR does not include results or information based primarily on judgement or on particular circumstances. This means, for example, that assessments of the level of environmental risk are not included nor are statements about the legal or commercial implications of the condition of the land.

As a second arm to the initiative, the working group recommended that LCRs be completed by accredited specialists in contaminated land, when these become available. The Institute of Environmental Management and Assessment (IEMA) is administering an accreditation process for specialists in land condition (SiLCs) for the purpose of taking responsibility for both information entry and verification. As criteria for accreditation, SiLCs may come from any of the disciplines involved in contaminated land and remediation, but must be:

▨ chartered or equivalent with at least 10 years' relevant experience

▨ able to demonstrate a high level of expertise within the processes involved with investigating and assessing contaminated land.

▶ **Land quality statements (LQSs)**

While land condition records concentrate on the collection and ordering of factual information, the commercial implications and real-estate issues arising from the development or acquisition of previously developed land or contaminated assets are dealt with in land quality statements (LQSs). These were provided for in the Royal Institution of Chartered Surveyors' guidance note, *Contamination and its implications for chartered surveyors* [25]. Key aspects are described in Appendix 11.

3.4.3 Action points on information handling

In the context of using LCRs and LQSs to assist in ordering and collecting records and information for scrutiny by third parties, the matters that should be taken into account are listed below.

1   LCRs and LQSs should be prepared by a specialist in land condition (SiLC) and a chartered environmental surveyor respectively, or by other appropriately qualified professionals.

2   Information collected should reflect all material facts.

3   The documentation collated should be expressly referred to in the contract of land sale or lease.

Further discussions on land condition records and land quality statements are included in Chapter 8.

First steps – site appraisal and acquisition

Chapter 4 covers the steps to be taken by the client before acquisition of the site. The client needs to deal with the appointment of key advisers. At the end of this stage the legal basis for site acquisition needs to be established, together with a funding strategy.

As a minimum, the client should carry out initial site appraisal having regard to taxation, building costs and potential remediation costs, planning costs and professional fees. Depending upon the nature of the transaction, however, and the client's policy on approaching site acquisition, more comprehensive information on site conditions may be required at this stage to reduce uncertainty and control risk.

While some transactions are unconditional, the guide concentrates on the more likely format of a conditional contractual arrangement or option. Possible levels of information required before agreeing the initial deal are discussed.

Key issues covered in Chapter 4

- appointing advisers
- site assembly and site ownership
- funding strategies
- opportunities for partnership support for regeneration
- identifying tax advantages
- legal issues
- risk transfer

- information required and level of detail needed – investigation strategies
- vendor's information
- waste
- achieving consistent reporting structures
- applications/consents/permits/licences
- health and safety
- developing the site log

4.1 KEY ISSUES FOR SITE APPRAISAL AND ACQUISITION

At this stage the client will have identified development opportunity and will have noted that the site is previously developed land.

As was clearly reinforced in *Releasing brownfields* [4], the financial viability of the project is the key issue. Initially, the way the various factors are to be built up should be assessed to inform the decision about whether or not the acquisition should proceed. As the process develops, these appraisals will be refined as more detailed information comes to hand. The subject areas to be considered as part of the appraisal include:

▶ *appointing advisers*

Selecting advisers is covered in Chapter 3 as part of formulating a development strategy. The advisory team needs to be appointed having regard to the elements of the specific project.

Refer to Chapter 3 and Appendix 3 for guidance on engaging advisers.

▶ *site assembly and site ownership*

The ease of acquisition is an important early appraisal issue. Land assembly issues are recognised in *Releasing brownfields* [4] as some of the key factors with all developments, particularly with previously developed land. Access to site assembly skills may be vital in assessing whether a project is viable. Single or multi-ownership sites present different issues.

Landowners may have false perceptions about the value of their land. Clients should also establish the presence of other interests, such as easements and rights of way.

Action points

→ Seek advice from property advisers as to whether the site is in single ownership or whether it needs to be assembled. If the latter, establish how this is to done.

→ Review whether the local authority needs to promote compulsory purchase powers to acquire the sites.

→ Ensure that the planning process does not hinge upon a single owner who could frustrate the scheme.

→ Establish whether the owner's aspiration of land value is misplaced and whether he is prepared to grant an option to give time to identify and manage possible constraints.

→ Review whether the total cost of acquisition can be justified within the financial appraisal of the scheme.

→ Establish whether other interests will complicate the process, eg easements, rights of way.

▶ *funding strategies*

The client should put in place a funding strategy. There is a multiplicity of structures for funding development and suitability will depend upon the client's commercial circumstances. Any funder will wish to quantify in financial terms the uncertainties associated with the site. CIRIA's report *Contaminated land – management of financial risk* [12] provides a detailed commentary on contaminated land-related financial risks and provision of finance.

Action points

→ Confirm that advisers are acceptable to funders.

→ Confirm that advisers will accept a duty of care to funders.

→ Check that adequate information is available to satisfy funders' requirements to undertake risk appraisals.

▶ *opportunity for partnership support for regeneration*

Partnership support for land and property regeneration schemes may be available from the regional development agencies (RDAs) and English Partnerships, the Welsh Development Agency in Wales and Scottish Enterprise in Scotland. In England, this can take the form of a brownfield improvement grant [26]; schemes of most interest to client developers cover:

■ propriety studies and small-scale short-term loans

■ direct development

■ gap funding for speculative development – where the developer is considered to be the beneficiary of the grant

■ gap-funding for bespoke development (ie where the end-user is known) – the occupier is considered to be the beneficiary of the grant.

For schemes in Scotland and Wales, the respective development agencies also have grant support mechanisms, which are subject to different terms.

Appendix 8 provides initial information on brownfield improvement grants. Appendix 10 shows contact points for the various development agencies. See also identifying tax advantages below.

Figure 4.1   *Canal with previously developed site*

Action points

→   Ensure advice may be obtained from financial advisers on opportunities.

→   Cross-refer information to your tax adviser.

▶ *identifying tax advantages*

Potential opportunities in respect of previously developed sites may include:

▪ **tax incentives for contaminated land**. The May 2001 Finance Act [27] enabled companies to claim 150 per cent of the qualifying expenditure on remediating contaminated land. The existence of the new tax relief is an added factor to be taken into account in negotiations between parties regarding the transfer of contaminated land. The Inland Revenue has confirmed that removal or treatment of asbestos in buildings will qualify for contaminated land tax relief.

Illustrative case study examples of tax relief calculations for different companies are given in Appendix 8.

▪ **VAT**. Companies should also consider the position on VAT on qualifying expenditure as to when or when not to elect for VAT in respect of the project. This is particularly important for refurbishment projects.

▪ **landfill tax exemptions**. Exemption from landfill tax may be a consideration for elements of the project. The law does not allow HM Customs and Excise to issue backdated certificates, and any waste removed before a certificate is issued will not be exempted from landfill tax. An application must be made 30 days before the developer intends to start removing the waste to landfill. The exemption is only obtainable if the reclamation of the land constitutes or includes clearing the land of pollutants that would (unless cleared) prevent the land being put to the intended use. Subject to other qualifying circumstances, asbestos waste cleared from buildings will qualify for landfill tax exemptions. See Example 4 in the landfill tax guidance note [62].

▪ **stamp duty**. From 30 November 2001, all property sales and assignments of existing leases for £150 000 or less that relate to land in the UK's most disadvantaged areas (specified in the regulations SI 2001/3747) have been exempt from *ad valorem* stamp duty. From the same day grants of new leases relating to land in disadvantaged areas have been exempt from *ad valorem* stamp duty on premiums of £150 000 or less.

The measure is designed to stimulate disadvantaged areas by attracting development and encouraging the purchase of residential and commercial property by individuals and businesses. SI 2001/3747 sets out a list of 1997 disadvantaged areas and SI 2001/3748 brings the provisions in Section 92 and Schedule 30 of the Finance Act 2001 into effect for documents executed on or after 30 November 2001.

The Inland Revenue website link provides a full list of these disadvantaged areas. See Section A10.5.

Action points

→ Obtain advice from tax advisers on opportunities afforded by current instruments.

→ For illustrative information on tax incentives (see Appendix 8).

→ Consult HM Customs and Excise for feedback and impacts for landfill tax exemptions.

→ Explore whether the brownfield improvement grant is a mechanism more suited to the development, should the project not qualify for the tax incentives highlighted.

→ Establish whether property is located in a deprived ward and qualifies for stamp duty exemptions.

▶ *legal issues*

The role of lawyers acting on the purchase of a previously developed site is the same as for other sites in that they endeavour to identify areas of liability that may affect their clients or the use and enjoyment of the property.

The Law Society's *Warning card on contaminated land* [28] makes it clear that all solicitors must consider contamination on every property transaction. Clients and advisers should refer to the text of the warning card – see Appendix 13.

While contamination may well be an issue on previously developed sites, it is only one of several specialist subjects that may need to be addressed. See Appendix 3.

Action points

→ Involve the specialist lawyers as early as possible in the process.

→ Ensure property lawyers possess, or have access to, appropriate specialist knowledge on environmental and planning law within the project team and if in any doubt call in an expert to work with them.

→ Check credentials of specialists (see Appendix 3).

▶ *risk transfer*

At the centre of the appraisal for any project on previously developed land is the assessment of risk and the manner in which the parties allocate risk between them. This involves the assessment of the present risk posed by the property and the legal agreement as to how the risk is managed. Risk may relate to contamination or other contractual or physical issues associated with the site. The major financial risk may not be contamination.

In the case of contamination, the site may be "contaminated land" under Part IIA EPA 1990 (see Chapter 2) or it may be contaminated but not so defined. The risk may, therefore, be compulsory clean-up, or a clean-up requirement arising upon the grant of planning consent.

In the case of land that is identified as contaminated land under the Part IIA regime, there are mechanisms for liability transfer:

- use by contractual negotiation of transferring liability to a purchaser by virtue of the exclusion tests set out in the statutory guidance accompanying Part IIA;
- provision under Part IIA for the parties to agree a liability apportionment in a contract and notify the regulator who may then, subject to certain conditions, follow the wishes of the parties. This is an "agreement on liabilities". See Paragraph D.38 of *Statutory guidance* (Annex 3 to Circular 02/2000[9]).

Action points

→ Agree precisely with legal advisers what risk may be accepted and for how long. Consider known and unknown contamination and establish triggers for responsibility.

→ Seek specialist legal advice on the application and operation of the exclusion tests and use of the "agreement on liabilities".

→ Ensure that liabilities are specifically addressed in leases as well as in purchase and construction contracts.

▶ *what information is required and in what detail – investigation strategies*

Chapter 3 emphasises the importance of planning to ensure rigorous management of data. At this initial stage, clients need to resolve how much information will be adequate to satisfy their decision-making procedures in acquiring sites.

The process is one of collecting information to build a conceptual model of the site and its surroundings, either in textual or pictorial form, to represent what is known at any given time about site conditions and their implications. The model can therefore be used as a means of identifying not only what is known but also what is required for decision-making and so act as a tool for planning the strategy of investigation.

BSI [29], recommends that from the outset an investigation strategy should be devised to meet given objectives. The process comprises:

- setting objectives for the investigation
- establishing the investigation strategy to meet these objectives
- obtaining the data
- reviewing the data
- determining whether or not it is sufficient to meet the planned objectives.

If this is not the case, then decisions need to be made as to whether the initial investigation strategy needs modification, eg employing more detailed investigation methods to obtain additional data.

Preliminary investigations, which comprise desk studies and site walkover inspections, form a valuable means of collecting initial data on the site from which broad assessments of the risks and implications that may be associated with the land can be made.

In certain circumstances, this level of information may well be sufficient to enable clients to make necessary decisions with requisite confidence. However, where this is not the case and further data is warranted, these preliminary techniques will have provided the initial contribution to creating the conceptual model upon which more extensive site investigations can be designed. Due care, therefore, needs to be taken to ensure such initial activities are undertaken effectively, and informed clients may find it advantageous to accompany their advisers at this stage.

For desk studies, there is a range of online services that will provide a considerable amount of site setting and environmental information relating to land at minimal cost. Further contact details are set out in

Appendix 10, although it is likely that professional advice will be required to ensure that the implications of such information are fully assessed.

The very nature of preliminary data-gathering is inevitably limited when compared with the results that can be obtained from detailed site investigation methods. Actual site data will greatly supplement the original information collected from desk studies and will increase confidence that the overall information package is indeed representative of the site conditions.

Case Study

Ignoring good practice approaches
Land purchase without appropriate enquiries

A housing developer bought a plot of land on which it planned to build a small number of private houses. No investigation into the background, site history or characteristics of the site was carried out.

After acquisition, substantial delays and costs resulted when the land was found to have been the site of a former gasworks. The developer had to pay, and wait, for additional investigations and scheme designs, which seriously eroded the profitability of the scheme.

Lessons learned

The lack of attention to good practice approaches, ie absence of desk study data, resulted in the developer incurring substantial loss of profit on the scheme.

The key issue is to establish the level of confidence needed in the information in order to make decisions. Clients may decide that to provide sufficient confidence for decision-making, further detailed intrusive investigations and related enquiries and consultations are needed to supplement the initial preliminary investigation methods.

Whether this decision is an overarching policy to be applied on all sites, or is dealt with site by site, governed, for example, by conditions placed on specific purchase negotiations, its resolution should be fed into the client's site acquisition strategy.

Case Study

Extent of investigations
Employing detailed site investigation at acquisition

Gas contamination was known to be an issue at a site being considered for acquisition. Only a proportion of the existing buildings on site had protective measures and the estimated cost of retro-fitting gas protection to the same standard in the remaining building threatened the deal.

The client commissioned specialist consultants who designed detailed investigations to identify both the source and the nature of the gas. As a result of the investigations, the consultants established that, other than provisions for sealing the points of service entry to building structures, no gas protective measures were required.

Lessons learned

By focusing on the critical issues, which also threatened to halt the purchase, the initial outlay on detailed investigation saved the client approximately 90 per cent of financial provisions that would otherwise have been necessary.

For the purposes of the structure of this client's guide, the issues and action points related to desk study and site walkover survey activity are covered in this chapter. Should there be a need for more detailed site investigation techniques at this site appraisal stage, clients need to refer to the relevant discussion/action points in Chapter 6 (Section 6.1) and introduce them at this stage.

Action points

→ Consider the amount of information required for site acquisition to maintain the quality of data collected and its subsequent management.

→ Refer to key guidance summaries for information on good practice approaches to data collection.

▶ *vendor's information*

In view of the exclusion tests contained in the statutory guidance in Part IIA (see Risk transfer above), vendors often provide a package of information that may include a site investigation of their own in an attempt to transfer liability to purchasers. Advisers need to be able to evaluate properly such information for both content and quality.

Action point

→ Provide advisers with all information provided by third parties.

▶ *waste*

Dealing with waste issues is covered in more depth in Chapter 7. Any implications on the viability of the site may need to be taken into account from this initial stage and be built into appraisals.

▶ *achieving consistent reporting structures*

For clients involved in several sites and acquisitions, a standardised presentation format for reports will assist the efficiency of the evaluation process.

Clients may have developed their own in-house format, but when this is not the case, many good practice guidance documents provide recommendations for structuring reports. For site investigations, British Standard 10175 [29] and the Environment Agency's guidance on site investigation [30] are examples of publications that include recommendations for the layout of investigation reports. The *Model procedures* documents produced by DEFRA [13] [14] [15] [16] and the Welsh Development Agency's *Manual* [31] are further examples of guidance on the structure of reports.

Clients with a portfolio of sites often engage a panel of advisers to provide similar services packages. Specifying a recommended good practice report template as part of the adviser's brief is likely to help limit differences in their approach and achieve better convergence in the structure of reports; this, in turn, will assist in their evaluation.

Action point

→ Establish adviser's approaches to adopting good practice procedures in producing and formatting reports.

→ Where a specific "client's report" format has been devised, ensure advisers are notified as part of the brief.

▶ *applications/consents/permits/licences*

Timely preparation is important in identifying requisite consents and having the ability to set realistic timetables for obtaining them. On the basis of activity on site at this stage consisting of a walkover survey, clients' obligations should be limited to obtaining requisite authority for entry to the site.

Where a client has resolved that there is need for more extensive (intrusive) investigation activity, further requirements for permits and licences will probably be triggered.

Chapter 6 gives further details. A summary table of permits and licences throughout the process is to be found in Appendix 7.

▶ *health and safety*

Figure 4.2   *Health and safety warnings on site gates*

The principles of managing health and safety issues on previously developed sites are essentially no different to those for projects in general. With previously developed sites, however, there is likely to be added potential for health and safety hazards. Should contamination be a potential feature that could cause harm, for example, to workers or the public, the circumstances must be properly addressed from the outset, as soon as access to the site is anticipated.

As the development unfolds and more extensive activities are undertaken for site inspections, detailed site investigations, and possible site demolition and remediation works, other issues with potential impacts on health and safety will have to be considered and managed. Typical situations are:

■ where, as a result of site operations, surface materials have been removed, leaving the underlying site materials exposed and creating a hazard because of previous uses or practices on the land

■ proximity to communities such as housing and schools, from where children may be able to gain easy access to the site

■ where the public assumes continued informal access and use of derelict sites.

A range of published guidance is available to communicate good practice and management of health and safety on sites and to set out the obligations of those involved. Guidance for contaminated sites forms a core of such publications, and many advisory and contracting organisations can demonstrate substantial experience and competence in this aspect. Appendix 3 offers prompts to clients about the need to establish the competencies of their advisers and contractors in health and safety matters. Health and safety is covered further in Chapter 6.

> **Action point**
>
> → Establish team members' experience and competence, including their approaches to applying good practice procedures and guidance for health and safety management.
>
> → Ensure health and safety is considered as a component of site planning, including initial access to the site, from the start of the project.

▶ *developing the site log*

Recommendations for devising and compiling the site log as a key repository of information are highlighted in Chapter 3. Creating the site log from the start of the project is essential to ensure initial data is captured and the possibility of misplacing later key material is minimised.

> **Action point**
>
> → Begin development of the site log (see Chapter 3 and Appendix 12).

4.2 KEY GUIDANCE

Department of the Environment

(1994) CLR2 *Guidance on preliminary site inspection of contaminated land*

(1994) CLR3 *Documentary research on industrial sites*

(1994) CLR5 *Information systems for land contamination*

(1995–1996) *Industry profiles*

[A series of publications describing specific industrial activity, listing contamination associated with each industry]

Department for Environment, Food and Rural Affairs

(2002) R and D Publication CLR8. *Potential contaminants for the assessment of land*

(In prep) and Environment Agency CLR11 *Handbook of model procedures for the management of contaminated land – overview*

(In prep) and Environment Agency CLR11 *Handbook of model procedures for the management of contaminated land, MP 1 Site assessment*

Department for Transport, Local Government and the Regions

(2001) and RICS Guide. *Partnership support for land and property development schemes. Direct development; speculative development and non speculative (bespoke development)*

Environment Agency

(2000)/NHBC R and D Publication 66. *Guidance for the safe development of housing on land affected by contamination*

(2000) R and D Project P5-065/TR. *Technical aspects of site investigation*, Vols 1 and 2

British Standards Institution

(2001) BS 10175, 2001. *Code of practice for the investigation of potentially contaminated sites*

(1999) BS 5930, 1999. *Code of practice for site investigations*

Chapter 4

Health and Safety Executive

(1991) *Protection of workers and the general public during development of contaminated land, HS* (G) 66

Construction Industry Research and Information Association

(1995) SP101 *Remedial treatment for contaminated land*, Vol I. *Introduction and guide*

(1995) SP103 *Remedial treatment for contaminated land*, Vol III. *Site investigation and assessment*

(2000) C545 *Land contamination – management of financial risk*

(2001) C552 *Contaminated land risk assessment – a guide to good practice*

Institute of Field Archaeologists

(1993 (revised 1999)) *Standard and guidance for archaeological desk based assessment.*

Institution of Civil Engineers

(1994) *Contaminated land: investigation, assessment and remediation. ICE Design Guide.* Thomas Telford, London.

National House Building Council

(1999) *Chapter 4.1 Land quality – managing ground conditions.*

RICS/Environment Agency

(2000) *Comprehensive project appraisal – towards sustainability.* RICS, London.

Welsh Development Agency

(1993) *WDA manual on the remediation of contaminated land.* WDA, Cardiff.

Interactions with planning

Obtaining planning permission without either unreasonable constraints or excessive planning gain is vital to maintaining the viability of regenerating previously developed land.

The aim of this chapter is to summarise the key planning issues and competencies that are relevant to obtaining planning permission for development of previously developed land.

Early consultation and discussion with the planning authorities and consultees helps to identify key issues that may affect associated with the development of the site.

Key issues covered in Chapter 5

Pre-application

- policy appraisal
- negotiations/discussions
- interaction between site investigation and planning
- how much detail will the planners require?
- emerging planning guidance

Formulating an application

- will an environmental assessment be required?
- will an "appropriate assessment" be required, or are there protected species on the site?
- scope of the planning application
- outline or detailed application?
- consultees on the application

5.1 INTRODUCTION

Figure 5.1 illustrates the interactions of the planning process with the general stages of development adopted in this guide.

In particular, it provides an indication of how the design phases of development interact with planning process, leading on to construction and post-construction activities providing the mechanism for conditions to be discharged.

Parallel discussions and consultations will inevitably be undertaken with bodies that may provide requisite authority, permits and consents. Appendix 7 provides a background summary illustration of consultations.

For the purposes of this *Client's guide*, this chapter refers to English guidance. Scottish, Welsh and Northern Ireland guidance documents are listed in Appendix 12.

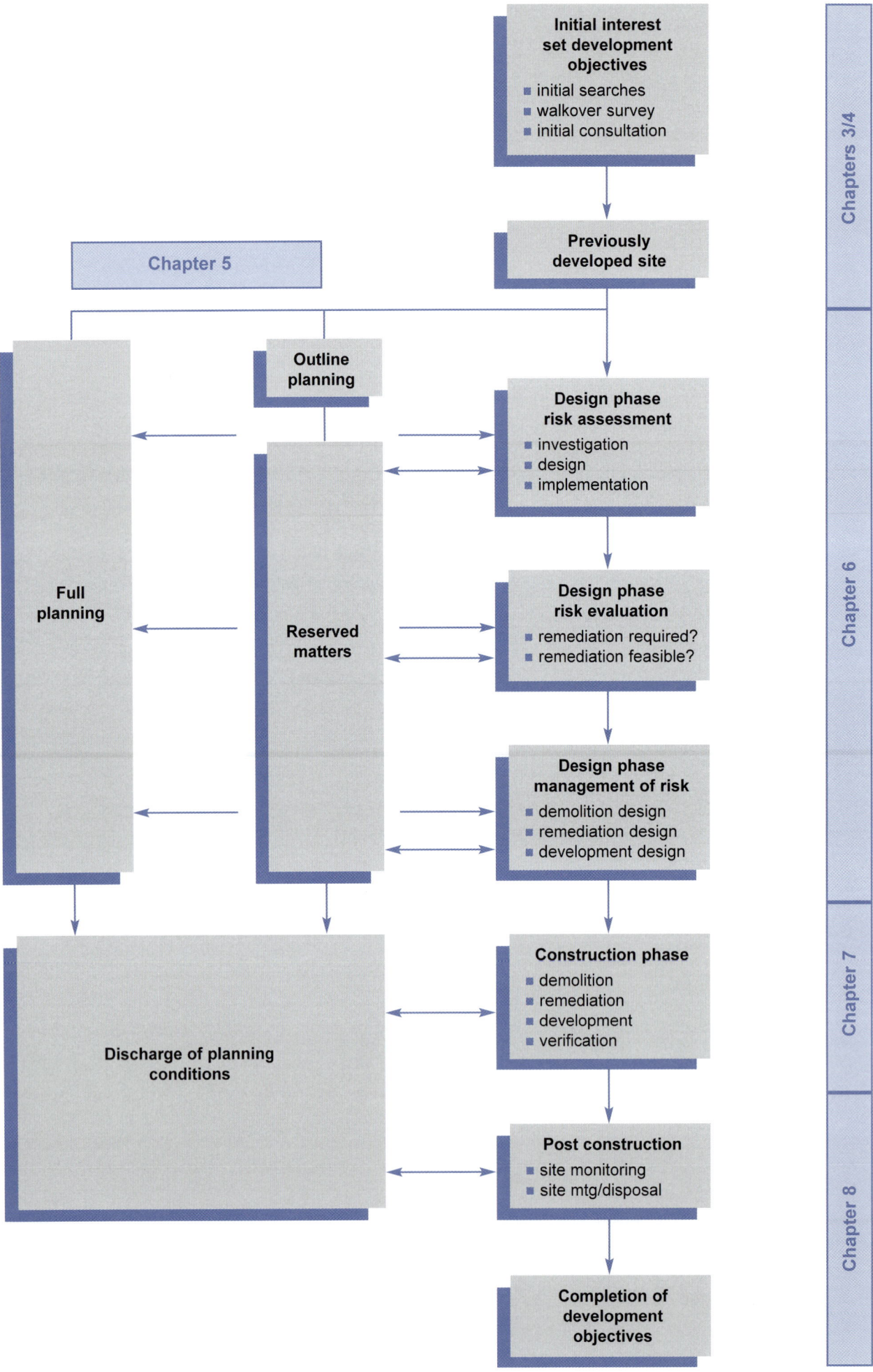

Figure 5.1   *Interactions with planning*

5.2 DEVELOPING THE PLANNING TEAM

Chapter 3 emphasised the importance of effective team selection and management for the successful development of previously developed land. Dealing with planning demands the same attention to detail in the assembly of the appropriate team, which may comprise:

- planning consultant/planning surveyor (in addition specialist expertise may be needed for transport, archaeology, community liaison or other matters)
- planning lawyer
- environmental consultant (specialist advice may be needed for areas such as ecology).

As with the development process as a whole, leadership of the planning team is a matter of choice, so practice varies. The client may have adequate in-house skills to lead the process or he may prefer this role to be assumed by a lawyer or a consultant. Overlaps in skills always exist in planning matters and it is important to demarcate areas of primary responsibility in setting up the team.

It is essential that team members hold frequent meetings.

Action points

→ Planning team members require planning, environmental and waste management expertise if they are to handle effectively planning applications on previously developed land.

→ The planning team should include expertise in developing community relations and managing local concerns.

→ Technical expertise with regard to infrastructure requirements is essential.

→ Design elements must be developed with sensitivity to the project envisaged.

→ Establish the project's viability given the obligations being entered into.

Typically, the planning application will be formulated by a combination of the client, the planning consultant and lawyer (with the environmental consultant acting as support in consultations) and with the planning consultant often handling the initial stages of submission and discussion.

A key point emphasised in this guidance is early planning and preparation; for planning, early involvement of legal advice can often repay dividends and is strongly recommended. This is important if the planning application is to comply with contractual obligations under a joint venture, option or sale contract.

5.3 THE PROCESS

Figure 5.1 illustrates the various stages and interactions likely to arise in the planning process. How these relate to the initial feasibility, detailed design, remediation and development planning will, of course, vary from project to project. A key component of the development of the client's management plan is one of establishing and planning how and when milestones, action points and relevant applications dovetail with the development process as a whole.

Chapter 3 and Appendix 5 provide further background on the formation of the client's management plan.

5.4 KEY ISSUES ASSOCIATED WITH PLANNING

5.4.1 Pre-application

▶ *policy appraisal*

With all jurisdictions, and with the fundamental importance of the development plan in achieving planning permission, detailed analysis of local and regional planning policy is key to success and will be undertaken by the client's planning consultant and/or lawyer.

The full impact of PPG 3 [1] may take time to emerge at the relevant local plan, but as a statement of government policy it will be a significant material consideration even without changes to the plan. However, there may be equally strong factors to be considered locally and there may be more than one option for local development on previously developed land. In addition, the use of previously developed land for commercial and mixed development may not be so appealing to a planning authority if residential targets are more important.

It is important that any urban capacity studies, planning statements or briefs, or particular areas or statements of interim policy are fully combined as part of the appraisal process. Chapter 2 summarises the role of Comprehensive Project Appraisal (CPA) [3] in providing an assessment method upon which to place a measure on the sustainability of a project. Many of the subcategories in the CPA provide opportunities that can act as a positive promotion vehicle for projects on previously developed land. It will be appropriate, therefore, to consider these issues in outline at this point. This will also help to identify requirements for consultations with relevant parties that may have associated interests, eg English Heritage and relevant bodies in Scotland and Wales.

Clients should also be aware that this evaluation process will progress as information and understanding of interactions develops throughout the project.

Action points

→ Establish local and regional policy drivers from the planning team.

→ As an applicant, ensure it is not assumed that planning permission will be granted pursuant to PPG 3 simply because it is to take place on previously developed land.

→ Establish whether the provisions of an adopted local plan pre-date or post-date current government policy.

→ Refer to Environment Agency/RICS Comprehensive Project Appraisal guidance or other recognised guidance (see Chapter 2).

▶ *negotiations/discussions*

Early discussions with planners will enable an applicant to factor in issues where local concerns are being voiced by either planners or residents. In larger cases, specialist public relations advice may be helpful at an early stage in dealing with these local issues, but care is needed in the use of such advice and applicants should not use intermediaries to detach themselves from the issues.

Government policy encourages greater participation of local communities in the planning process. Applicants will need to be sensitive to this when dealing with local interests.

In some cases, the revival of the use of land will be viewed as positive by local opinion, but the key to successful planning is an appreciation by planners and local residents of the true financial cost of development on potentially contaminated and difficult sites. Local non-governmental organisations (NGOs) may also have concerns, however, on the wider issues relating to development, for example, introduction of social housing into the scheme. Taking all aspects into account, it is for the client to make out the overall case.

Managing schemes on previously developed land
Insufficiently detailed remedial strategies fuelling concerns of local action groups

Submissions of an insufficiently detailed remedial strategy for the development of a former manufacturing factory and a local action group's concerns over the redevelopment of the site led to it becoming a political issue. Initial investigations and the proposed remedial strategy were perceived to be insufficient and were rejected by the local authority. A revised strategy was then produced and eventually approved by the local authority one year after the original submission. However, during this period, the redevelopment of the site had become a focus of local concern about construction of new housing in the area. A local action group remained unhappy about the council's decision and felt that its concerns had not been answered. An appeal to the local MP led to the involvement of the DETR and the Environment Agency.

Lessons learned

Considerable effort had to be made to communicate risks and bring round local opinion. This included introducing a series of measures to improve communication for the duration of the development, including a hot-line to consultants and regular liaison with the residents' association on the development site.

Research and consultations in *Releasing brownfields* [4] reveal developers' concerns about certain planners' lack of experience and understanding of previously developed land issues. Planners may feel that developers exaggerate the difficulties to avoid further planning gain. A balance must be struck, based on unambiguous factual material presented in a clear and concise fashion by the developer.

In view of the uncertain timescales associated with environmental assessment, applicants should obtain from planning authorities as early as possible indications of the need for, and scoping of, the environmental statement. It may also be appropriate to start to establish the parameters for any transport or retail studies that may be required.

Discussions should also take place at this stage with all consultees relevant to the project. See Chapter 3.

The applicant may find it necessary to clarify specific points of detail to planners as part of the application process.

If any environmental licence or authorisation is required, the applicant may wish to instigate that process at this time to run in parallel with the planning process. Early consultation with environmental regulators is essential.

Depending upon progress through the development process, key educational support tools may include:

- exhibitions and meetings
- executive summaries of the application
- non-technical summaries of any environmental assessment
- non-technical summary of site investigations
- summary of physical conditions and significant development hurdles
- submissions as to appropriate conditions.

Where documentation is involved, some of these may be combined in a single document. The overriding key is simplicity and transparency whilst ensuring that all relevant information is provided to ensure that

Chapter 5

non-technical summaries do not result in a distorted picture. SNIFFER's guide, *Communicating understanding of contaminated land risks* [32], provides guidance on communication issues.

> ## Action points
>
> → Undertake discussions with key consultees.
>
> → As part of the application process, clarify specific points of detail as necessary to planners.

▶ *interaction between site investigation and planning*

Existing guidance for planning authorities for dealing with contaminated land (PPG 23 Part 4 and Annex 10) pre-dates the Contaminated Land (England) Regulations 2000. New draft technical advice on planning and contaminated land will be published in due course by DTLR [10]. Until its publication, the current general principles still apply. Basic points include:

- the responsibility for providing information on whether it is contaminated rests primarily with the developer
- the authority needs to know "whether the proposal takes proper account of contamination"
- certain issues are the responsibility of other environmental regulators
- if contamination is known or strongly suspected then investigation and remediation proposals will generally be required
- local authorities may impose conditions on the site investigation process.

Although sites with low levels of contamination may be appropriate candidates for conditions only, it is likely that in most cases and for most future uses a full site investigation is likely to be required by the planning authority before a planning application will be considered.

Key references include:

DETR Circular 02/2000 [9], *Contaminated land – implementation of Part IIA of the Environmental Protection Act 1990.*
This mentions interaction between the Part IIA regime and planning and development control. It does not replace PPG 23 [33] but does say that the expression "*contaminated land*" in PPG 23 "*should be interpreted in the general sense rather than according to the particular definition used for the purposes of the Part IIA regime*".

When considering a planning application where contamination is an issue then, under the *suitable for use* approach, risks should be assessed, and remediation requirements set, on the basis of both:
- the current use and circumstances of the land
- its proposed new use.

DOE Circular 11/95: The use of conditions in planning permissions [34]

This prescribes the criteria for the formulation of planning conditions. It contains model conditions for when a remedial scheme is agreed before planning permission is granted and also for when soil contamination is known or suspected but no investigation has yet been undertaken.

DOE Circular 1/97: Planning obligations [36]

Any request for a Section 106 Agreement should be judged by the guidelines set out in this Circular. An agreement should not be required where conditions can adequately cover issues, unless unusual circumstances exist.

The Planning Green Paper [35]:

The Planning Green Paper *Planning: delivering a fundamental change* [36] represents the first step in a comprehensive review of the planning system. For further detail see emerging planning guidance below.

> **Action point**
>
> → Clarify and confirm key reference documents with planners.

▶ *how much detail will the planners require?*

If there is no history of potentially contaminative uses nor any subsequent indications of any contamination upon initial inspection, the planning authority may accept a desk study (Phase I) report as evidence of the position. The draft Technical Advice Note on planning and contaminated land [10] states (at paragraph 30):

> 30. *LPAs should pay particular attention to the condition of the land where the proposed use of the land 'would be more vulnerable to any past contamination; or where the current circumstances or past use of the land suggest that contamination may be present, or where it has relevant information. Full account should be taken of whether the proposed use or development for which planning permission is being sought is capable of being adversely affected by contamination, if any. For example, contamination is unlikely to be relevant if the proposal is to add a new storey to an existing building.*
>
> (Draft DTLR Technical Advice Note, Para 30) [10]

The LPA may, however, impose conditions as to further investigation or relating to the discovery and notification of problems during the development process.

In view of the responsibilities of local authorities under Part IIA and the danger of the clean-up of orphan sites falling on the public purse, some local authorities may take an unduly cautious and prescriptive approach to the overall process. The impact of this must be balanced against the financial viability of the scheme.

If the planning authority requires an intrusive investigation, then, as discussed in Chapter 6, careful consideration is needed about the form this report should take. Technical rigour needs to be integrated with effective communication of the results.

If possible, an agreed methodology should be discussed with the planning authority to avoid repeat work. In some cases planning authorities may lack the expertise and be reluctant to instruct external advisers. It will then be incumbent upon the client or adviser – for example, an environmental consultant – to advise upon a methodology. In common with the theme of this guide, the report should follow a robust methodology incorporating accepted good practice.

The form of the report should be considered in draft and discussed with other members of the team to determine presentational issues. Consultants engaged for this aspect should have the expertise to produce clear and concise conclusions comprehensible to non-expert planners and committee members.

Again, endorsing the recommendations in Chapter 3 on the advisability of preplanning report needs, clients should endeavour to ensure that a site investigation can be used for all purposes for which such a report is required. For example, not only should agreement be established with planners on the consultants who are to be commissioned and the proposed methodology that is to be employed, but these should also be agreed with any funders.

The site investigation reports should also be adequate to assist any environmental assessment processes, waste management licence surrender issues on the site and/or act as a baseline for a new application for a permit under the Pollution Prevention and Control (England and Wales) Regulations 2000 [55].

> **Action points**
>
> → Establish planners' requirements on extent and methodology of investigation (see also Chapter 3).
>
> → Confirm constitution of advisory team with planners and funders (see also Chapter 3).
>
> → Review and identify the scope and overall requirements of investigation.

▶ *emerging planning guidance*

At the time of going to press three items of significant policy guidance were being developed in relation to planning and contaminated land and these are:

■ *Draft technical advice note: Development on land affected by contamination* [10]

This will supersede the advice currently contained in PPG 23 [33] (relating to planning and contaminated land). It is hoped that the advice will be consistent with the concepts of "significant harm" and the "significant possibility of harm" contained in Part IIA. Early drafts suggest that it will be emphasised that planning considerations and the range and type of receptors are different for planning and include some things excluded from Part IIA such as the impacts of radioactivity and waste licensing. Practitioners and developers will be keen to ensure, however, that compliance with Part IIA requirements satisfies the technical requirements of local planning authorities even if broader amenity issues relating to the development as a whole need to be considered separately.

■ *Draft Environment Agency internal guidance on planning application responses relating to "Land contamination – Part IIA and the planning regime"* [11]

This sets out the manner in which the Environment Agency should respond to planning consultation for sites that are or may be contaminated. It makes reference to the Agency's Better Town Planning Project and the Environmental Protection Priority Planning Exercise. The guidance contains a number of model conditions and informatives, particularly for special sites, where the Agency has greater responsibility. It emphasises that under Part IIA only the current use is considered, whereas under planning regard can be had to current and proposed uses. Where no determination has been made under Part IIA that land is "contaminated land" the Agency's involvement will be restricted to controlled waters and waste issues. If pollution of controlled waters is identified, however, the Agency should inform the local authority to enable the land to be formally designated.

■ *The Planning Green Paper*

The Planning Green Paper *Planning: delivering a fundamental change* [35] was published in December 2001. This is to be followed by a number of specialist "daughter" consultations to consult upon specific elements of the proposals. Papers have already been published on compulsory purchase, planning obligations and reform of the Use Classes Order.

Users of the guide will be aware of many of the proposals as they are finalised through primary legislation, regulations and guidance. The new provisions will affect the advice contained in this guide, but the extent of this is unknown. Reference to the client's specialist advisers will enable the client to be fully informed on these matters. Among the proposals is the introduction of the following.

1 Local development frameworks to replace local plans and unitary development plans.

2 New arrangements for community involvement in preparation of the local development framework and in significant planning decisions.

3 Simplification of the hierarchy by strengthening regional planning and abolishing structure plans.

4 Measures to reduce the volume and complexity of national planning guidance.

5 Measures to speed up planning by setting new targets for applications and appeals.

6 Performance standards for consultees with right to charge fees.

7 The use of checklists for applications.

8   More master planning of major schemes.

9   Business planning zones.

10   Measures to prevent twin-tracking and repeated applications.

11   Limits on planning consents to three years.

12   Increased planning fees to fund better performance.

13   Rejecting the need for third-party appeal rights.

14   More transparency with planning obligations.

15   Reviews of compulsory purchase procedures.

5.4.2   Formulating the application

▶ *will an environmental assessment be required?*

The answer will relate to the type of development proposed as the end use. Should it be required under the Town and Country (Environmental Impact Assessment) (England and Wales) Regulations 1999 [38] and related sets of regulations, some issues will need to be addressed for developments on previously developed land.

In some cases it may be advisable for those involved in undertaking the site investigation, eg the environmental consultant, to be involved in production of the environmental statement (ES), but only if the adviser has adequate expertise in this field. This may form a criterion for selection of the team.

Schedule 4 to the Regulations sets out the required contents of the ES and includes:

> *a description of the physical characteristics of the whole development and the land use requirements during the construction and operational phases.*

The end use of the development will have impacts of its own. The current status of the site is also an important issue to be considered. Perceived dangers of previously developed sites, from a public perspective, are likely to involve the impact of the actual development process on the surrounding environment, eg during a major clean-up operation, or demolition, that may involve substantial excavation and interaction with water resources.

> **Perceptions will exist of potential exposures to harmful substances and materials and the ES needs to address these issues carefully.**

Care is needed not to exceed the statutory parameters of the scope of an ES, local environmental problems and the manner in which they are resolved can assume disproportionate significance in the process. Nevertheless, the formulation of a good case on these matters can ease the planning path.

Action point

→   Review project team capability/selection when environmental statements are required.

▶ *will an "appropriate assessment" be required, or are there protected species on the site?*

Early consultation with the relevant statutory conservation organisations and the local authority, as well as legal pre-contract enquiries, should have identified whether the development site forms part of, or is likely to have significant effect upon, a site or species protected under the Conservation (Natural Habitats etc) Regulations 1994 [39]. If this is the case it is likely, although not certain, that an environmental statement will have been requested under the 1999 Regulations. In England, the appropriate assessment under the 1994 Regulations is carried out by the planning authority or by the secretary of state in consultation with English Nature.

Applicants should refer to the guidance set out in PPG 9 [40] and to the guidance published by the European Commission in dealing with the requirements of Article 6 of the Habitats Directive 92/43/EEC.

In addition, certain species are protected under other legislation, and licences are required to disturb or relocate them. Such licences may or may not be granted. Examples include badgers, bats and great crested newts, which are often present in urban locations.

Action points

→ If development is likely to have an impact upon protected sites or species, applicants should consider whether this is likely to prevent development of any type and should not contract other than upon a conditional basis.

→ Obtain specialist environmental and ecological advice in considering the significance of such issues (as above).

→ Do not assume that an urban location is free of such problems. (In fact it might be the opposite and sites may be a safe haven as a result of dereliction.)

▶ *scope of the planning application*

Large parts of the application will be concerned with the buildings or new development to take place on the land. In general this guide does not deal with those matters but concentrates specifically on issues relating to previously developed sites.

The new development will be the principal component of any application, but for previously developed sites other parts of the proposal need to be included within the development description, such as:

■ demolition and removal of buildings and underground structures

■ engineering and excavation related to remediation schemes

■ waste storage on site and reuse of waste materials

■ potential for contaminant mobilisation

■ mobile plant for on-site remediation

■ mobile plant for recycling/crushing of materials for potential use as secondary aggregate

■ permission for *in-situ* remediation.

In exceptional cases, planning and building regulation approval may interact, eg if buildings are being designed specifically to handle the possibility of gas venting where complete remediation of a site is impractical.

Although some of these elements may be implicit within the application, it is preferable to make them explicit. Any ambiguity could lead to a new permission being needed, causing delay to the project.

Action points

→ Establish communication with Building Regulations and the Environmental Health department of the local authority.

→ Clarify and confirm scope of application to avoid ambiguity.

► *outline or detailed application?*

Discussions should take place with the local planning authority to decide whether the application should be outline or full. This issue may also be relevant to contractual arrangements. There is little point in submitting an outline application under a contract arrangement if the local planning authority requires a detailed application where, for example, the consent is required for a waste management licence or PPC permit.

It is possible for land contamination to be dealt with as a reserved matter in an outline consent. If there is a possibility that contamination has off-site implications, or if several different operations need permission, then a full application may be preferable. If detailed monitoring and aftercare are significant issues, a planning agreement may be required, but simple arrangements can be dealt with by condition.

Action points

→ Establish whether PPC permits and/or waste management licences are required.

→ If planning and other environmental authorisation processes are to proceed in tandem, ensure that appropriate professional advice is obtained so as to avoid excessive overlaps and to maintain consistency in controls.

► *consultees on the application*

The principal consultees that are likely to be concerned with the issues arising from development on previously developed land are listed in Chapter 3.

Case Study

Regulatory consent
Liaison with regulatory bodies

A former steelworks that closed in the early 1990s was the subject of a private-sector purchase with the objective of achieving comprehensive remediation and optimum redevelopment. A planning application for reclamation and redevelopment was submitted in 1997.

Planning consent was granted with conditions. However, delays in assembling the funding package for the scheme resulted in the work not being implemented. The site owners and their partners remained committed to the scheme, but a review of the proposals during this delay period led to the regulatory bodies requesting more stringent conditions. New legislation and different perceptions of risk formed the basis of these revised conditions.

Notwithstanding the thorough assessment of the scheme during the preparation of the planning application, regulatory officers used the delay to introduce a more stringent analysis of risks and added supplementary conditions to the consent.

Lessons learned

Access to a formal protocol for liaison between project promoters and regulatory bodies would have provided a more robust framework for scoping the risks and addressing relevant issues at the outset. (The development agency and the regulators involved with the scheme have as a result pursued the creation of a formal protocol for grant-funded reclamation projects.)

5.5 KEY GUIDANCE AND POLICY DOCUMENTS

Some of the policy documents and guidance relevant to planning applications for previously developed sites are set out below.

> For development in Scotland and Wales, reference must be made to appropriate relevant planning guidance.
>
> For Scottish, Welsh and Northern Ireland documents, refer to Appendix 12.

White Paper *Our towns and cities: the future – delivering an urban renaissance*
(reference has already been made to government policy including related initiatives)

Planning Policy Guidance Notes

PPG 1   *General policy and principles*

PPG 3   *Housing*

PPG 9   *Nature conservation*

PPG 10   *Planning and waste management*

PPG 11   *Regional planning*

PPG 12   *Development plans*

PPG 14   *Development on unstable land*

PPG 23   *Planning and pollution control*

PPG 25   *Flood risk*

Draft Technical Advice Note

Development on land affected by contamination
Draft for consultation

Regional Planning Guidance Notes (RPGs)

DETR Circulars

(1995) 11/95   *The use of conditions in planning permissions*

(1997) 1/97   *Planning obligations*

(2000) 02/2000 *Environmental Protection Act 1990: Part IIA: Contaminated land.*

Environment Agency

(2002) *Land contamination, Part IIA and the planning regime.* Draft internal guidance on planning application processes.

Environment Agency/RICS

(2001) *Comprehensive project appraisal – towards sustainability.* RICS, London.

Scotland and Northern Ireland Forum for Environmental Research (SNIFFER)

(1999) Project Number SR 97 (11) F *Communicating understanding of contaminated land risks.*

Design phase

Chapter 6 covers issues relevant to the design and specification phase of building on previously developed sites. The detailed stages consist of:

- detailed site investigation (including implementation) to:
  - gather information on the site conditions
  - undertake risk assessments on the implications
- detailed design of demolition
- detailed design of potential remedial measures
- detailed design of the development itself taking due account of the fact that remediation provisions can be integrated and proposals are "buildable".

The potential interactions and overlaps between the stages were described in Chapter 3. This design stage is pivotal to the process with possible overlaps with:

- site purchase acquisition (Chapter 4)
- planning issues (Chapter 5)
- providing the evolving background for taking forward the construction procurement and implementation (Chapters 7).

At these detailed design stages, consultation and communication will take on a significantly higher profile. Various bodies act as consultees to the planning regime with potential overlaps with consultations on requirements for health and safety of workers, occupants and the impacts on the public and the environment.

Key issues covered in Chapter 6

- reviewing advisers
- technical good practice issues
- nature conservation
- archaeology
- engaging contractors for investigation
- embracing sustainable development criteria
- consents/permits/licences
- waste
- health and safety
- managing environmental protection
- the need for site monitoring
- communicating and consulting with third parties

- data management – developing the site log
- reports
- continuing communications and consultations – reports
- designing the remediation strategy
- integrating of the remediation strategy with development planning and design
- landfill tax and landfill tax exemptions
- communicating proposals and consulting with planners/consultees/regulators
- integrating the remediation strategy with development planning and design

6.1 KEY ISSUES FOR SITE INVESTIGATION, DESIGN, IMPLEMENTATION AND RISK ASSESSMENT

Detailed site investigation, coupled with risk assessment, is the precursor to the detailed design stages of development. With these design phases being key decision-making phases in the development process, the effectiveness of information gathering and the associated assessments is crucial. Figure 5.1 illustrates the relationships between undertaking investigation and detailed design of the components of development.

Geotechnical issues and their impacts will be a major investigation objective. A further objective will be the gathering of data to establish or refute that circumstances exist, taking into account situations created by planned new uses where there are unacceptable risks caused by contaminant sources being linked to site receptors.

The initial desk study and walkover stages will have been directed to identify possible linkages. Detailed investigations can help determine whether circumstances do give rise to such unacceptable risks. Where this is the case, it triggers the remediation design phase, comprising measures that address such risks.

Site investigation can be a time-consuming and costly exercise, and the project team needs to be chosen with care.

The programming and detailed content of investigations relating to the stages of the development process will be subject to the client's commercial priorities. Clients with, for example, appropriate contractual safeguards in place, may decide that it is not necessary to undertake detailed investigation to characterise the site until the detailed design phase. Others may consider that obtaining detailed information is a necessary part of their decision-making in acquiring sites and bring forward these processes to the site acquisition stage (see Chapter 4).

The time needed to undertake the investigation process, from design and discussion with regulators, to site activity, laboratory testing and reporting, should not be underestimated, and realistic provisions need to be made and built into the project programme. Should there be a need to obtain planning permission in relation to the scope of certain investigations, this can result in substantially greater provisions having to be allowed in the project programme.

When detailed investigations are undertaken (and given the levels of investment that may be involved in obtaining the data), it is important that information obtained is of a quality that will permit it to be incorporated into later design and evaluation processes.

▶ *reviewing advisers*

Two issues need to be borne in mind in reviewing advisers' continuing capability to provide support to the project:

- advisers' capability. Chapter 3 highlighted the potential for understanding of the characteristics of previously developed sites to change as information is obtained. New information may make it necessary to modify the overall portfolio of skills of the project team. Advisers may already possess these skills, but where they fall outside their scope, clients will need to ensure that there are provisions to review the advisory team to supplement expertise, should it be required

- expectations of third parties. As noted in Chapter 4, clients may find that various interested parties, who they may need to satisfy, have particular requirements in respect of advisers. This should also be taken into account when reviewing the project team.

Action points

→ Establish with advisers how they will communicate situations where their capabilities are unable to match site circumstances.

→ Take account of the requirements of other parties who may be involved in the project as they relate to advisers.

▶ *technical good practice issues*

A comprehensive range of good practice guidance exists on detailed investigation techniques.

The following are key checkpoints that clients should ensure are adequately covered:

- objectives and purpose of the investigation. These should be clearly established before the start. Examples would cover investigation to:
  - collect site characterisation information
  - defend a position

- collect design information for site remediation
- evaluate cost
- undertake site valuation

■ *past activity*. Any information on past activity on the site – investigation, remediation or provisions in former development construction – should be taken into account. See case study below

■ *vicinity of site*. The process of collection of information needs to allow appropriate account to be taken of conditions in the vicinity of the site that may either:
- be affected by the site itself, or
- have an effect on the site

■ *investigation to be representative*. The planned programme of investigation, sampling and testing needs, so far as may reasonably be foreseen, to be representative of the potential site characteristics to be encountered

■ *combined investigations*. The opportunity to take advantage of combining geotechnical (eg information for subsequent foundation design for the development itself) and geoenvironmental investigations has been fully considered. Certain geotechnical characteristics are also relevant to the assessment of risks from contamination. AGS's guidance document, *Guidelines for combined geoenvironmental and geotechnical investigations* [41], discusses these issues

■ *phasing of investigation*. Whether undertaking investigations on a phased basis is subject to constraints of time (to exploit possible opportunities to rationalise and improve efficiency) is appropriate

■ *QA/QC*. Quality assurance and quality control procedures should be in place to cover the components of investigation. See Appendix 4 for summary information on national accreditation schemes for contractors and laboratories

■ *environmental protection*. Design and implementation of site works should take into account provisions for environmental protection and provision should be made for emergency contingency plans for environmental incidents (see Management of environmental protection in this chapter and CIRIA's handbook [42])

■ *relevance of sampling and testing*. Where contamination is concerned, designs and specifications for the sampling and testing of contaminants need to be consistent with:
- the site conditions anticipated and described by the conceptual model for the site
- the criteria to be used to evaluate the site. For example, nationally derived contaminant guideline values may well be employed as the criteria by which the impact of measured site contaminant levels are judged. These guideline values will have been derived using assumed testing procedures for contaminants. Specifications for site work need to be consistent with the basis upon which such evaluation criteria have been established. As an example, the Environment Agency has set out proposed requirements for laboratory performance [43]

■ *health and safety*. Appropriate provisions are in place. See Health and safety in this chapter

■ *information presentation*. The structure/content of reports needs to be developed in an appropriate format (see Section 3.4).

Chapter 6

Inadequate site investigation
Departure from good practice

A housing developer commissioned a geoenvironmental site investigation following acquisition of a site. The investigation comprised a small number of boreholes, from which the developer's advisers concluded that site conditions were "suitable for housing".

Contrary to good practice, a desk study was carried out after the investigation and revealed the site had previously been used as a gasworks and a vehicle depot.

The client's advisers did not review the original advice relating to the suitability of the site for housing, the potential for contamination to be encountered or for the need for precautions/ potential remedial works during construction.

During subsequent construction, a tar tank was encountered. This halted construction and caused a six-month delay in the programme while further investigation was carried out to establish the conditions at the site and to redesign the housing layouts.

Lessons learned

Clients need to:

- pay due regard to competency of appointed advisers
- ensure that their advisers are not working beyond their core skills or areas of expertise.

Action points

→ Establish whether design and specification criteria for investigation processes are in accordance with good practice and whether any departures are justified.

→ When land is to be investigated through intrusive investigation take into account circumstances, particularly in sensitive situations, where future control of the activities may not be possible, eg where investigation is undertaken before a site purchase that may not necessarily proceed.

→ Ensure good practice environmental protective measures are not only in place, as with all activities, but also ensure the provisions and eventual use are properly documented.

▶ *nature conservation*

When planning a site investigation, clients should recognise that proposed investigation works might affect protected species on the site. Derelict buildings may be havens for rare species. Issues relating to permissions are dealt with in Section 6.2.

The investigation design and planning process should take this aspect into account.

Action point

→ Check that appropriate provisions are built in to identify and then manage the presence of protected species on site as part of investigation design and implementation

▶ *archaeology*

As with nature conservation, clients should ensure that there is appropriate provision for establishing and managing any archaeological issues that may arise.

Action point

→ Check that appropriate provisions are built in to identify, and then manage, the presence of archaeological issues as part of investigation design and implementation.

▶ *engaging contractors for investigation*

Guidance on selection and engagement of investigation contractors is provided in Appendix 4. Key issues are:

■ expectations of third parties. As with the selection of advisers (see above), clients may find that third parties with an interest in the site also need to vet contractors

■ consistency of the investigation package. Irrespective of how clients' investigation contractors are engaged – whether through direct engagement or via commissions by advisers – clients should establish that the services provided include a component that contributes to a consistent and seamless overall package. This may involve ensuring that work on site, related laboratory support and subsequent interpretation of results all dovetail together without any discontinuities or gaps.

Action point

→ Obtain confirmation from the project team that the investigation package is consistent and complete.

→ Take into account the requirements of relevant parties involved in the project in regard to changing contractors.

▶ *embracing sustainable development criteria*

Section 2.3.1 summarises the role of *comprehensive project appraisal* (CPA) [3] as an assessment method by which the sustainability of a scheme may be measured. Many of the subcategories in the CPA can act as positive drivers for projects on previously developed land.

Clients should be aware that the process of evaluating sustainability criteria will begin as soon as information and better understanding of its interactions with criteria relevant to the scheme are first obtained. Major interfaces between CPA criteria and the scheme as a whole will occur during design and implementation of remediation and development. By opening up this area in outline at this point, however, clients will be better able to make early identification of necessary consultations with parties that may have particular issues, eg English Heritage.

Action point

→ Consider the relevance of components of the scheme against sustainable development criteria.

▶ *consents/permits/licences*

Clients should be aware that with potentially contaminated sites, specific agreement might be needed with the environmental agencies on approach, where investigations are planned and where potentially vulnerable water resources either underlie or are local to the site. Regulators are likely to require consultation and agreement on matters such as methods of investigation (eg borehole construction details) and be satisfied that agreed site procedures will be complied with.

The range of contacts relevant to the key permits and licences for site investigation activities is described in Appendix 7.

▶ *waste*

Dealing with waste issues is covered in depth in Chapter 7.

▶ *health and safety*

The principles of managing health and safety on previously developed sites are essentially no different to other projects. Clients have a duty to check that those who may be involved in operations have competency and experience in dealing with health and safety issues. However, with such land there is potential for additional hazards to health and safety.

The primary health and safety legislation that applies to projects on previously developed land comprises:

- Health and Safety at Work etc Act (1974) [22]
- Management of Health and Safety at Work Regulations (1999) [44]
- Construction (Design and Management) Regulations (1994) [23]
- Control of Substances Hazardous to Health Regulations (COSHH) (1999) [45]
- Construction (Health Safety and Welfare) Regulations (1996) [46]
- Construction (Design and Management) Regulations 1994: Managing Health and Safety in Construction, Approved Code of Practice (2001) [72].

Other regulations may also apply when specific materials are present on sites. For example, lead and asbestos regulations may be relevant.

Clients should also be aware that in areas where there may be a need to gain access to abandoned or live mine workings for inspection, surveying or eventual construction activity, the health provisions of the Management and Administration of Safety and Health at Mines Regulations 1993 apply [47]. The interfaces with CDM Regulations need to be established when this is the case.

For previously developed sites, specific issues of relevance are:

- structural stability of buildings
- stability of earth slopes/retaining walls, hazards from voids and cellars
- hazardous materials either on site or remaining in buildings
- hazardous materials contained within the fabric of buildings
- live site and building services
- redundant services ducts or pipes containing hazardous materials
- the security of the site.

Ground investigations need to comply with the requirements of the CDM Regulations. A planning supervisor and principal contractor may therefore be required as part of the project team. Depending upon the duration of the investigation and the number of persons involved, the HSE may have to be notified of the activity. Key factors to be taken into account in planning, designing and specifying investigations include:

- complying with health and safety regulations, eg undertaking the designer risk assessments, health and safety plans, associated with design and implementation of investigation
- putting into place emergency/contingency planning to cater for circumstances that are not necessarily anticipated from current site data
- taking into account and managing disturbed and/or exposed site materials as a result of the investigations that may otherwise cause hazards to receptors, eg to children, or to drains or streams through contaminated runoff from the site, or to local air quality from dust.

▶ *managing environmental protection*

CIRIA's guide *Environmental good practice on site* [42] provides an effective entry into the required provisions and approach covering management responsibilities, environmental management planning, training and the role of environmental management systems.

In addition to the various recommendations of the CIRIA guide, particular provisions may be needed where contaminated land is encountered, in order to manage the risks of cross-contamination of soils and/or groundwater. For example:

■   if boreholes are inappropriately designed, they can act as preferential pathways for the movement of contamination

■   inappropriate filling and sealing of redundant boreholes can lead to the creation of preferential pathways

■   where precautions have not been put into place there may be potential for the contamination of streams or rivers; for example, stockpiles of site materials exposed to rainfall may cause subsequent contaminated runoff into watercourses.

▶ *the need for site monitoring*

Clients should be aware that, in certain circumstances within an investigation, longer-term monitoring may be required. This may arise in situations where site conditions are suspected to be changing with time or where it is suspected that existing conditions may be affected by subsequent development activity. Two typical situations comprise the need for monitoring to identify either continuing or reducing migration of groundwater contamination or to establish the migration characteristics of soil gases.

Advisers may recommend monitoring programmes as a part of site evaluation to track fluctuations in conditions (eg to groundwater levels) over time. It may also be a condition of planning for the site, to demonstrate compliance with imposed planning conditions. Monitoring may, therefore, either form part of the investigation itself or help establish trends in current site conditions. The technique can have wider applications, too; for example, where there is a need to establish the longer-term implications of site development and the effects of site remediation.

In such cases, the initial investigation creates the information baseline against which later data can be compared. Consistency between the initial and subsequent information collection methods is vital, to ensure that results can be compared accurately and to avoid wasting initial expenditure.

Chapter 6

► **communicating and consulting with third parties**

As part of the investigation, there should be effective communication and consultation with third parties.

Formal consultees to the planning process can be involved (see Chapter 5). In addition, investigation activities often affect sites that have, for example, been unoccupied for a considerable time and been colonised with wildlife. Other third parties should also be considered, therefore – neighbouring owners, occupiers, community and conservation interest groups and societies, for example. Well-informed neighbourhood groups sometimes have their concerns aroused by the degree of attention being given to protective measures for nearby residents.

Clients may also benefit from communication channels of this kind by gaining further intelligence about the site, for example, through personal recall of past site activities from longstanding local residents. Any such consultation should, however, be undertaken with care and sensitivity to guard against leaving such groups with misconceptions.

Case Study

Breakdown in communications arouses concerns of active local residents and causes avoidable disruption to site activities

The concerns of a local residents' action group were aroused when site investigation began on a closely neighbouring site without any notice. Their chief concerns related to the adequacy of planned measures to manage dust and the resulting risk of exposure to dust-borne substances. Site activities were delayed as a result of the residents' concerns and demands for independent specialist representation to look after their interests and review the otherwise sound precautions in place for the management and control of site activities.

Lessons learned

Failing to communicate planned intentions and activities can result in significant disruption to activities.

Action points

→　Identify pressure and interest groups and establish communication channels.
→　Utilise contacts for further information gathering on site history.

► **data management – developing the site log**

Information from investigations is likely to be extensive and should be captured in the site log as soon as practicable (see Section 3.4). Additionally, data can be developed and collated into documents comprising the statutory provisions of the health and safety file under the CDM Regulations.

Action point

→　Co-ordinate investigation data into the site log.

▶ **reports**

The potential range of reports that may be generated at this stage as a means of communication are listed in Appendix 11.

> **Action point**
>
> → Liaise with advisers on setting requirements for reports.

6.2 KEY ISSUES FOR DEMOLITION AND DECOMMISSIONING DESIGN

Demolition and decommissioning may be a highly significant (and specialist) component of dealing with previously developed sites.

Figure 6.1 *Example of decommissioning work at an old gasholder*

▶ **reviewing advisers**

Demolition and decommissioning of existing operational plant, structures or buildings are specialist issues, and advice should be obtained before undertaking work of this type. Advisers providing such services should be able to demonstrate competence and experience covering:

- assessment of stability of structures and design of any stabilising works
- the handling of hazardous materials
- specific materials, eg asbestos
- special wastes
- implications of live services
- related health and safety measures
- related environmental protection provisions.

Certified demolition contractors can often provide access to specialist demolition design advice.

► *consents/permits/licences*

As for investigation, a summary of potential requirements for demolition/decommissioning is set out in Appendix 7.

► *health and safety*

In common with investigation, the CDM Regulations apply to demolition processes and designs, and the specification should take this into account. With demolition design phases, the development of a pre-construction health and safety plan will be needed as part of the support documentation for procuring a demolition contractor.

► *managing environmental protection*

Design and specification for demolition should take into account good practice in environmental protection [42]. For a summary of the key issues refer to Section 6.3 Key issues for remediation design.

► *waste*

Implications of waste need to be taken into account at this stage. Dealing with waste issues is covered in depth in Chapter 7.

► *nature conservation*

As with site investigation, it may be necessary to deal with impacts upon protected sites and upon species on previously developed sites. Derelict buildings may be havens for rare species. Quite apart from the need to obtain appropriate licences and permission for the development to proceed, the impact upon cost and timing of the development needs to be considered at design stages and taken forward to construction. Issues that could arise include:

■ the need for site boundary demarcation and protection to minimise impacts upon adjoining or nearby protected sites

■ the need to fulfil obligations arising from an environmental impact assessment or planning conditions

■ impacts because of cost and timing of protective or relocation measures to protect fauna (eg seasonal issues relating to bats and newts)

■ making allowance for contingencies, such as impacts on the project timetable, should protected species be discovered during the works.

► *archaeology*

As with nature conservation, there may be impacts associated with archaeological issues. The impacts, costs and timings of investigations need to be considered at the design and construction stage.

> **Action point**
>
> → Check that appropriate provisions are built in to identify and manage the presence of archaeological issues on site as part of demolition design.

► *communicating and consulting with third parties*

As recommended for site investigation (Section 6.1 above), communication and consultation channels with third parties should be maintained throughout the demolition and decommissioning phases.

► *embracing sustainable development criteria*

Clients can now consider sustainable development principles within the project in greater depth (see Section 2.3). While many of these principles are likely to attach positive value to the development, clients should be aware that they may give rise to constraints that will have to be balanced against the benefits.

Examples would be possible effects on project programme, limits or restrictions that may occur on overall scheme design or on the overall flexibility that may be applied to site operations, eg to ensure appropriate protective measures are in place. Potential areas where sustainability criteria may be relevant are:

■ *materials reuse and recycling*

Previously developed sites can offer a wide range of demolition materials for reuse and recycling. The aggregates tax [60] may also contribute to the financial benefits of this approach. It is important to define the criteria for rejecting potentially reusable materials, eg due to their condition or because of contamination. This will assist in defining the methods by which such materials will be monitored and verified as suitable for reuse or otherwise

■ *heritage*

The affect of any planned demolitions on the harmony of local heritage, buildings and/or sites of historic significance

■ *noise/vibration*

Management of night-time/daytime noise etc from site operations

■ *conservation/biodiversity*

Maintenance and sensitivity of contributions of existing land condition

■ *transport*

Management of traffic movements/traffic noise.

> **Action points**
>
> → Undertake sustainability appraisal in accordance with recognised methodologies such as Environment Agency/RICS comprehensive project appraisal [3].
>
> → For planned reusable and/or recycled materials, set out verification/rejection criteria.

▶ **data management – developing the site log**

As with previous stages, the site log should include aspects that relate to design; see Section 3.4. This demolition design stage may also include provision for dealing with aspects of remediation, eg removal and disposal of special wastes.

Action point

→ Develop the site log for forward planning interactions between demolition and site remediation activities.

▶ **continuing communications and consultations – reports**

Appendix 11 lists the range of potential reports that may be generated at this stage as the means of communication.

6.3 KEY ISSUES FOR REMEDIATION DESIGN

Figure 6.2 *Housing development built on a brownfield site*

▶ **reviewing advisers**

The key issues relating to advisers' capability are discussed in Section 6.1 Key issues for site investigation design, implementation and risk assessment.

▶ **designing the remediation strategy**

Development schemes need to be tailored to the specific circumstances of each site. Devising the appropriate site remediation solution is a multi-disciplinary process that should embrace:

■ the practical integration of the proposals within the development itself

■ the basis of how completion of the project is defined

■ constraints due to construction programme/future site management

■ project cost planning

■ communication of proposals to the regulators

■ acceptance of proposals by third parties.

Remediation strategies should be devised from the technical options available. It essential to identify clearly the criteria defining the extent of remediation. Clients need to be satisfied not only that the selected treatment option will be effective on site, but also that it will be compatible with the site's wider surroundings and its proposed development.

Guidance is available on the selection of remedial measures in Environment Agency [15], which provides a framework for comparing and selecting a strategy from available options. Among the criteria covered are:

- applicability – to deal with contaminants
- availability – status of development and track record
- treatment costs
- treatment duration
- operational requirements – eg working area, access to site, services, environmental impact, monitoring
- effectiveness – in respect of any inherent limitations
- flexibility – to adapt to circumstances and to integrate with the development
- post-treatment – management and/or monitoring commitments after completion of treatment process.

An aspect that is likely to be of growing relevance as part of the selection of remedial options is whether the implementation of site remediation can itself be considered part of the overall sustainability of the development. The reduction in risks and the benefits resulting from the treatment, such as those to human health and/or the environment, can be compared with the costs and the impacts that the actual remediation activities may create, such as transport movements or risks to local residents.

Collating detailed documentation and records of the process is essential. As part of site reporting, a remediation strategy management plan, setting out the principles and approaches behind the design and direction to back-up data, can provide an invaluable tool at this design stage. This can lead to a developing record of activities. Guidance on the remediation strategy plan is given in *Model procedures* MP 3 [16].

Action points

→ Establish criteria to be used in selection of the treatment option.
→ Develop a remediation strategy document for continuing scheme management.
→ Establish interaction of sustainability of remediation within the overall project evaluation.

▶ *integrating the remediation strategy with development planning and design*

Clients should take care to ensure that the selected remediation design will integrate with the proposals for development to ensure that the overall scheme design is a buildable solution and will remain so in the face of future plans for modification etc.

The practicalities of development design often result in late changes in final site layout. An inflexible remediation strategy may create avoidable problems. It is essential that careful thought be given to the long-term integrity of the remediation strategy. For example, where clients have plans for future modifications, the implications for the future performance of the planned remediation should be considered.

Remediation design and that of the development should not be considered as independent activities since specific components of the eventual development design may often form part of the overall remediation strategy of the site.

For example, cover materials specified for open spaces or access hard standings may have been designed to act with specific properties, to support soft landscaping or vehicle loading, respectively. They may also have specific roles in contributing to the remediation solution, by providing a designated interface acting as a barrier between users of the site and the underlying site materials, or an impermeable surfacing that can direct rainfall to drainage and thereby counter the effects of infiltration that may otherwise transport contaminants to underlying groundwater.

Where interactions occur between development planning and remediation solutions, they need to be understood by the parties involved to ensure the overall development scheme remains technically sound.

Action points

→ Ensure communication links are in place between project team members to cover interactions of the relevant design disciplines.

→ Put in place means by which implications of design changes on remedial strategy can be reviewed.

▶ *requirements for consents/permits/licences*

Initial consultations or actual applications for consents etc that may be activated for remediation design activities is set out in the table in Appendix 7.

▶ *landfill tax and landfill tax exemptions*

It is essential to factor the cost of landfill tax into overall disposal costs payable as construction is undertaken. It must not be forgotten, either, that exemptions are also relevant for the disposal of certain wastes arising from the reclamation of contaminated land. The extent of materials that may be applicable will be a matter for discussion with the tax office in question. To establish a valid appraisal of project finances, it is vital to distinguish between those wastes that will or will not qualify for exemption and the consequent impact on costs.

The principal preconditions are:

■ reclamation must involve clearing the land of pollutants that are causing harm or have the potential to cause harm

■ the cause of the pollution must have ceased

■ the land is not subject to a works notice in connection with the provisions of the Water Resources Act 1991 [49] or a remediation notice in connection with the Part IIA regime (see Appendix 2)

■ in the case of reclamation for development, the reclamation constitutes or includes clearing the land of pollutants that would (unless cleared) prevent the land being put to the intended use

■ landfill tax exemptions extend to materials within buildings that are contaminated. Exemptions may also apply to buildings situated on contaminated land that have to be demolished so that the underlying materials can be treated. Establishing the detailed criteria for "qualifying" materials is best resolved with HM Customs and Excise. Potential issues to be resolved are foundations and services installations.

Action points

→ Clarify who is to be responsible for applications for landfill tax.

→ Consult Customs and Excise Guidance Note 2 (LFT 2) (see Chapter 7 Construction phase).

→ Establish with the tax office the basis of the extent of "qualifying" materials.

► **waste**

Implications at this stage need to be taken into account. Dealing with waste issues is covered in more depth in Chapter 7, Construction phase.

► **health and safety**

Health and safety management issues affecting site investigation (Section 6.1) are relevant to remediation stages as well. For instance, designer's risk assessments and health and safety plans will need to be provided for and developed for inclusion into design documents prepared for the construction phase. Risk assessments under the COSHH Regulations [45] will be required, too.

As also highlighted for investigation in Section 6.1, where site remediation activities incorporate work governed by the Mines and Quarries Act 1954 and Mines and Quarries (Tips) Act 1969 [48] [50], provisions for managing health and safety will need to be suitably tailored.

Action point

→ Establish nature of remediation activities and legislation as may be relevant to health and safety.

► **managing environmental protection**

Remediation design and specification should take into account good practice in environmental protection. CIRIA's guide *Environmental good practice on site* summarises the issues [42]. Dust and/or water quality monitoring should cover conditions before demolition starts (benchline conditions), and should continue thereafter to establish the level of impacts as construction takes place.

► **nature conservation**

Action point

→ Consult CIRIA's guide on environmental protection [42].

As with site investigation and demolition stages, it may be necessary to deal with impacts on protected sites and species on previously developed sites. The main issues are set out in Section 6.2.

Quite apart from the need to obtain appropriate licences and permission for the development to proceed, the effect on cost and timing of the development should be considered at design stages and taken forward to construction. Issues that could arise include:

■ the need for site boundary demarcation and protection to minimise impacts upon adjoining or proximate protected sites

■ the need to fulfil obligations arising from an environmental impact assessment or planning conditions

■ impacts because of cost and timing of protective or relocation measures related to species protection (there may be seasonal issues relating to bats or newts, for example)

■ allowing for contingencies, such as the effect on the project timetable should protected species be discovered during the work.

> **Action point**
>
> → Ensure impacts of potential nature conservation are built into remediation design and specification and project programming.

► *archaeology*

As with nature conservation, archaeological issues may have to be taken into account. The impacts, costs and timings need to be considered and taken forward into the construction stage.

> **Action point**
>
> → Ensure that impacts of potential archaeological issues are built into remediation design and project programming.

► *communicating proposals and consulting with planners/consultees/regulators*

The remediation design process involves consultations and discussions with the authorities to establish agreement on remediation strategy. This will lead to agreements on the discharge of any conditions attached to planning permission.

The authorities are likely to require submissions that incorporate details of proposals. Probable headings are likely to include:

- the form of remediation:
  - proposed activities
  - contaminants to be addressed
  - site areas involved/dealing with interfaces at property boundaries
- provisions for site management/supervision
- project monitoring provisions
- site verification/definition of project completion:
  - testing procedures and criteria to be employed
- programming/phasing
- waste disposal activities
- classification/volumes
- imported materials
- health and safety provisions
- environmental protection provisions.

Other parties may require similar information with related consultation. For residential sites, for example, clients seeking NHBC warranties are likely to be obliged to submit similar packages of information.

> **Action point**
>
> → Identify consultees relevant to the development scheme and their respective requirements for information submissions.

▶ **communication and consulting with third parties**

Section 5.4.1 highlights the need to ensure communication channels with third parties have been opened effectively. These should be maintained.

Action point

→ Maintain and consolidate communication channels with third parties.

▶ **embracing sustainable development criteria**

Chapter 2 summarises Comprehensive Project Appraisal [3] and its role in assessing project sustainability. In common with the demolition stage, sustainable development criteria can also be considered as components of remediation design. While the CPA categories highlighted for demolition (see Section 6.2) are relevant to this site remediation stage, additional CPA categories may now become important. Examples that may arise at this stage are:

- improving water quality of surface/groundwater
- improving land by remediation.

Case Study

Extent of investigations

Remediation works on a public-private sector investment initiative involving the development agency, borough council and landholder involved the successful treatment of land containing expansive slag material with a potential for differential ground heave. The remediation was designed using a risk management-based approach, employing appropriate site investigation data and probability-based risk assessment.

Lessons learned

Based on a detailed understanding of ground conditions and a quantitative probability-based risk assessment, the remediation design has allowed the vast majority of expansive material at the site to be used in a sustainable and cost-effective way. The partial depth treatment of the whole site:

- eliminates the requirement for off-site disposal of expansive slags
- minimises the need for imported material.

Action point

→ Undertake sustainability design appraisal in accordance with recognised methodologies such as Environment Agency/RICS comprehensive project appraisal [3].

▶ **data management – developing the site log**

As with earlier activities, the thinking and actions behind remediation design need to be recorded to ensure the overall design concepts are retained. Here again the site log acts as the key repository of information from which other reports can be written (see below).

Action point

→ Maintain the site log.

▶ *reports*

Appendix 11 lists the range of reports that may be generated at this stage as a means of communication.

6.4 KEY ISSUES FOR DEVELOPMENT DESIGN

▶ *reviewing advisers*

The effective dovetailing of remediation design with development design will be crucial to the viability of the project. The project team should be able to understand the interactions and implications and be properly briefed.

Action points

→ Ensure the project team is properly briefed on the interactions between remediation and development design.

→ Seek confirmation that design issues fall within their respective spheres of competence.

▶ *consents/permits/licences*

A look-up table for the potential range of consultations at this development design stage is included in Appendix 7.

▶ *integrating the remediation strategy with development planning and design*

Section 6.3 highlighted the need to ensure that the overall scheme is technically viable, emphasising that remediation provisions should be flexible enough to avoid being compromised by development design changes.

In the context of development design (and where remediation has been identified), designs also need to be compatible with such provisions. Where final scheme designs have to be substantially altered, clients should ensure that their advisers take account of associated modifications to remediation to ensure the overall strategy is not compromised.

Action point

→ Check that advisers are appraised of the continuing need for project design to integrate with remediation provisions.

▶ *health and safety issues*

Development design affects wider areas of building and infrastructure construction, as do the related health and safety matters. On sites where remediation is a component, clients should ensure the members of their project teams have been made fully aware of how and where development design and remediation design interact.

Remediation can be programmed in advance of development construction. In this situation, a key factor for following construction activities will be the conditions on the site after remediation – the residual conditions.

For this subsequent activity, the project health and safety file will be a vital reference document to record this information and upon which to build robust construction procedures.

Alternatively, remediation can be co-ordinated with construction. In this case, the client should seek assurance from the project team that it is devoting appropriate attention and management to the interface of remediation with development in the often-dynamic situation on site.

> **Action point**
>
> → Ensure advisers are giving sufficient importance to health and safety in respect of possible interfaces between development and remediation.

▶ *management of environmental protection*

CIRIA's guide [42] provides advice on good practice.

> **Action point**
>
> → Check that advisers are appraised of the continuing need for project design to integrate with remediation provisions.

▶ *waste*

Dealing with waste issues is covered in more depth in Chapter 7. Implications at this stage need to be taken into account.

▶ *nature conservation*

Requirements for dealing with nature conservation were described in Section 6.2. Similar considerations need to be covered during this development design stage.

> **Action point**
>
> → Ensure impacts of potential nature conservation are built into development design and project programming.

▶ *archaeology*

As with nature conservation, there may be impacts relating to archaeological issues. See Section 6.2 for discussion of the issues.

> **Action point**
>
> → Ensure impacts of archaeological issues are built into development design and project programming.

▶ *communicating proposals with planners/consultees/regulators*

The factors described for remediation design in Section 6.3 are also relevant for the development design stage.

▶ **communicating and consulting with third parties**

As with communicating proposals with planners (above), refer to Section 6.3 for issues associated with third parties.

▶ **embracing sustainable development criteria**

The design phase for the final site development again affords opportunity to build upon the sustainability of the project. See Chapter 2 for the outline summary to comprehensive project appraisal [3].

Depending upon the site, further sustainability criteria to those listed in Section 6.3 may be relevant:

- redevelopment of land:
  - brownfield site redevelopment in preference to greenfield sites
  - the reuse of contaminated land
- industry type:
  - contributions to the existing diversity of different industry types
  - contribution to overall industrial development
- environment:
  - enhancing the existing nature, beauty of the landscape
  - building in aesthetic features.

Action point

→ Undertake sustainability appraisal in accordance with recognised methodologies such as Environment Agency/RICS Comprehensive Project Appraisal [3].

▶ **reports**

Reports that may be generated at this stage as means of communication are listed in Appendix 11.

▶ **data management – developing the site log**

As with remediation design, development of the site log will facilitate access to the interactions between development design and the remediation strategy.

Action point

→ Continue development of site log. Refer to Appendix 11.

6.5 KEY GUIDANCE

The range of good practice guidance in this area is extensive. Initial references are provided below.

6.5.1 General – all stages of design

Department for Environment, Food and Rural Affairs

(In prep) and Environment Agency CLR 11 *Handbook of model procedures for the management of contaminated land – overview*

(In prep) and Environment Agency CLR 11 *Handbook of model procedures for the management of contaminated land – MP 1 Site assessment*

(In prep) and Environment Agency CLR 11 *Handbook of model procedures for the management of contaminated land – MP 2 Selection and evaluation of remedial measures*

(In prep) and Environment Agency CLR 11 *Handbook of model procedures for the management of contaminated land – MP 3 Implementation of risk management measure*

(2002) and Environment Agency R and D Publication CLR 7 *Assessment of risks to human health from land contamination: an overview of the development of soil guideline values and related research*

(2002) and Environment Agency R and D Publication CLR 8 *Potential contaminants for the assessment of land*

(2002) and Environment Agency R and D Publication CLR 9 *Contaminants in soil: collation of toxicological data and intake values for humans*

(2002) and Environment Agency R and D Publication CLR Tox 1 *Contaminants in soil: collation of toxicological data and intake values for humans. Arsenic*
[One of a series of publications, CLR Tox 1, Tox 2 etc, describing toxicological data for specific contaminants]

(2002) and Environment Agency R and D Publications CLR 10 *The Contaminated Land Exposure Assessment (CLEA) model: technical basis and algorithms*

(2002) and Environment Agency R and D Publication CLR SGV 1 *Soil guideline values for arsenic contamination*
[One of a series of publications, CLR SGV 1, SGV 2 etc, describing soil guideline value data for specific contaminants]

Department of the Environment

(1987) ICRCL 59/83 *Guidance on the assessment and redevelopment of contaminated land*, 2nd edition

Scotland and Northern Ireland Forum for Environmental Research (SNIFFER)

(2000) *Framework for developing site specific risk assessment criteria for human health risk assessment for contaminated land*

(1999) Project Number SR97(11)F *Communicating understanding of contaminated land risks*

Scottish Environment Protection Agency (SEPA) and Environment Agency

Pollution Prevention Guidance Notes (PPG(**))

(1999) PPG 5 *Works in, near or liable to affect watercourses*

(1998) PPG 6 *Working at construction and demolition sites*

Health and Safety Executive

(1991) *Protection of workers and the general public during development of contaminated land*, HS (G) 66

Construction Industry Research and Information Association

(1995) SP111 *Remedial treatment for contaminated land. Vol XI Planning and management*

(1999) C502 Coventry, S and Woolveridge C, *Environmental good practice on site*

(1996) R132 Steeds, J E, Shepherd, E and Barry, D L, *A guide for safe working practices on contaminated sites*

Welsh Development Agency

(1993) *WDA manual on the remediation of contaminated land*. WDA Cardiff

6.5.2 Site investigation

Department of the Environment

(1994) CLR4 *Sampling strategies for contaminated land*

(1995–1996) *Industry profiles*
[A series of publications describing specific industrial activity, listing contamination associated with each industry]

(1987) ICRCL 59/83 *Guidance on the assessment and redevelopment of contaminated land*, 2nd edition

Environment Agency

(In prep) *Monitoring Certification Scheme (MCERTS) to the chemical testing of soils*

(2000) R and D Technical Report P5-065/TR *Technical aspects of site investigation, Vols 1 and 2*

(2000) R and D Technical Report P5-066/TR *Secondary model procedure for the development of appropriate soil sampling strategies for land contamination*

(2001) NGWCLC Report NC/99/38/2 *Guide to good practice for the development of conceptual models and the selection and application of mathematical models of contaminant transport processes in the subsurface*

Construction Industry Research and Information Association

(1995) SP103 *Remedial treatment for contaminated land. Vol III Site investigation and assessment*

(1993) R131 *The measurement of methane and other gases from the ground*

(2001) C552 *Contaminated land risk assessment – a guide to good practice*

Association of Geotechnical and Geoenvironmental Specialists

(2000) *Guidelines for combined geoenvironmental and geotechnical investigation*

British Standards Institution

(1999) BS 5930:1999 *Code of practice for site investigations*

(2001) BS 10175:2001 *Code of practice for the investigation of potentially contaminated sites*

British Drilling Association (BDA)

(1992) *Guidance for the safe investigation by drilling of landfills and contaminated land*

British Urban Regeneration Agency

(2001) *Breaking old ground: BURA guide to contaminated land assessment and development*

Institution of Civil Engineers

(1993) Site Investigation Steering Group (1993) *Specification for ground investigation*, Thomas Telford, London

Scottish Enterprise

(1998) *How to approach contaminated land*. Scottish Enterprise, Glasgow

(1998) *How to investigate contaminated land*. Scottish Enterprise, Glasgow

6.5.3 Demolition

Construction Industry Research and Information Association

> (1995) SP102 *Remedial treatment for contaminated land. Vol II Decommissioning, decontamination and demolition*

British Standards Institution

> (1982) BS 6187 *Code of practice for demolition*

6.5.4 Remediation design

Department of the Environment

> (1994) CLR 1. *Framework for assessing the impact of contaminated land on groundwater and surface water*

Environment Agency

> (2001) *Guidance on the application of waste management licensing to land remediation activities Version 2.0*

> (2001) *Guidance on the disposal of contaminated soils*, Version 3

> (In prep) Project P5-046. *Supporting guidance for the verification of risk assessment and risk management measures*

> (2000) R and D Technical Report P5-035/TR/01 *Assessment and management of risks to buildings, building materials and services from land contamination*

> (2001) NGWCLC Report NC/99/38/2. *Guide to good practice for the development of conceptual models and the selection and application of mathematical models of contaminant transport processes in the subsurface*

> (2000) R and D Publication 95 *Guidance on the assessment and monitoring of natural attenuation of contaminants in groundwater*

> (1999) R and D Publication 20 *Methodology for derivation of remedial targets for soil and groundwater to protect water resources*

> (1999) ConSim: *Contamination impacts on groundwater – simulation by Monte Carlo Method.* Report in conjunction with Golder Associatcs (UK)

> (1999) Technical Report P316 *Cost benefit analysis in remediation of contaminated land*

> (1994) NRA R and D Note 301 *Leaching tests for the assessment of contaminated land*

> (1999) *Policy and practice for the protection of groundwater*, 2nd edition

> (2000) *Costs and benefits associated with the remediation of contaminated groundwater: a framework for assessment*

> (2000) R and D Technical Report P307 (P3-055) *Technical support materials for the regulation of radioactively contaminated land*

> (2001) NGWCLC Report NC/99/73 *Piling and penetrative ground improvement methods on land affected by contamination: initial technical guidance on pollution prevention*

> (In prep) Project P5-039 *Guide on short term risks to human health*

> (In prep) Project NC/66/07 *Methodology for comparison of CLEA with other human health risk assessment packages*

> (In prep) Project P5-041 *Guidance on site specific assessment of chronic risks to human health from contamination*

> (In prep) R and D Technical Report P338 *Assessing risks to ecosystems from land contamination*

Scotland and Northern Ireland Forum for Environmental Research (SNIFFER)

(2000) Report SR 999) 02F *Framework for deriving numeric targets to minimise the adverse human health effects of long term exposure to contaminants in soil*

(1996) Report SR 3846/1 *Ecological risk assessment manual for chemicals in the aquatic environment*

Construction Industry Research and Information Association

(1995) SP104 *Remedial treatment for contaminated land. Vol IV Classification and selection of remedial methods*

(1995) SP106 *Remedial treatment for contaminated land. Vol VI Containment and hydraulic measures*

(1995) SP107 *Remedial treatment for contaminated land. Vol VII Ex-situ remedial methods for soils, sludges and sediments*

(1995) SP108 *Remedial treatment for contaminated land. Vol VIII Ex-situ remedial methods for contaminated groundwater and other liquids*

(1995) SP109 *Remedial treatment for contaminated land. Vol IX In-situ methods of remediation*

(1996) SP124 *Barriers, liners and cover systems for containment and control of land contamination*

HM Customs and Excise

(2001) Guidance Note 2 (LFT 2). *Reclamation of contaminated land*

6.5.5 Construction design

Environment Agency

(2000) R and D Technical Report P5 035/TR/01 *Assessment and management of risks to buildings, building materials and services from land contamination*

Construction Industry Research and Information Association

(1992) SP 79 Hartless, R, *Methane and associated hazards to construction: a bibliography*

(1998) SP 134 Coventry, S, Guthrie, P, *Waste minimisation and recycling in construction – design manual*

Building Research Establishment

(1995) BRE Report BR 291, Paul V, *Bibliography of case studies on contaminated land: investigation, remediation and redevelopment*

Construction phase

This chapter provides clients with prompts to assist them in the construction phases. It:

- provides guidance to identify competent contractors for previously developed

- assists clients in recognising factors that need to be considered to ensure the construction process not only dovetails with the design stages, but is itself self-contained.

Chapter 7 considers:

- procurement of construction:
  - identifying competent contractors
  - bringing forward design stage factors into the construction procurement stage

- implementation of construction:
  - management and control of construction works.

In particular, many environmental issues will have been included in the tender and related risks and responsibilities will have to be allocated both before and during the construction phase. Such issues should form part of the employer's requirements and should be monitored once a contract begins.

Key issues covered in Chapter 7

Procurement – pre-qualification

- project management
- pre-qualification enquiries for contractors

Procurement – setting employers' requirements

- establishing how activities in the construction phase are to be verified
- construction insurance
- incorporating design issues
- incorporating planning conditions
- site co-ordination issues
- setting obligations of contractors
- nature conservation
- accommodating specialist contractors
- waste management
- landfill tax exemptions
- water pollution

- health and safety
- data management – developing the site log

Implementation

- reviewing advisers
- is the selected remediation strategy compatible with development planning and design?
- verification
- environmental protection
- consents/permits/licences
- sustainable development criteria
- communication with planners/consultees/regulators
- communications and consultations with third parties
- landfill tax exemptions
- reports

7.1 KEY ISSUES FOR CONSTRUCTION PROCUREMENT: PREQUALIFICATION

▶ *project management*

Releasing brownfields [4] highlighted that a crucial component behind successful development of previously developed land is access to experienced and effective project management. This is identified as one of the criteria for selecting advisers in Appendix 3 and as projects move to the construction stage, authoritative project control becomes a major factor.

Figure 7.1   *Excavation and disposal work on a contaminated site*

▶ ***pre-qualification enquiries for contractors***

Using pre-qualification to establish contractors' policy and approaches can provide valuable insight into their competence. It provides the baseline for evaluating responses from contractors to the specific needs of a project when formal procurement processes are undertaken.

Increasingly, development pre-qualification requires a degree of environmental competence even for projects not related to previously developed land. A higher degree of expertise in handling potential risks is now required. In relation to previously developed land these issues are of central importance to the successful conclusion of a project and impact directly upon the economics of a scheme. In addition, there is a requirement for an understanding and interface with health and safety requirements under the CDM Regulations and others that may apply – see Chapter 6.

Examples of enquiry topics are set out in Appendix 4.

7.2 KEY ISSUES FOR CONSTRUCTION PROCUREMENT: SETTING EMPLOYERS' REQUIREMENTS

▶ *establishing how activities in the construction phase are to be verified*

Verifying that construction-phase activities have been satisfactorily undertaken is essential. In developing documents for procuring construction, the requirements for verification of the activities need to be considered in detail. Verification has particular importance for:

■ the administrative control of the project itself

■ providing the transparent mechanism for establishing that any related obligations have or are being been accomplished, eg the satisfactory discharge of planning conditions

■ satisfying future occupiers/users of the site.

For many of the activities relating to building and infrastructure construction, familiar processes such as site supervision, along with materials testing and inspection, are employed to establish that progress of the works is satisfactory and completion is achieved.

With remediation activities, and depending upon the nature of the project, verification should be undertaken to identify:

■ that satisfactory progress is being achieved, eg at interim stages, indicating in turn that satisfactory completion of remediation should be achieved at a given target date; and/or

■ that satisfactory completion of remediation has indeed been achieved.

Each site is unique. The combination of the remediation processes employed, the performance criteria the processes are designed to achieve, site characteristics, such as geology, hydrogeology site history and current usage all contribute to a specific situation. Verification processes, therefore, need to be tailored to account for the site-specific nature of the project.

Detailed guidance on verification of remedial measures is in preparation by the Environment Agency [51].

Action point

→ Ensure that verification criteria and related procedures that are developed through the design and planning stages are built into the construction stages.

▶ *construction insurance*

The most appropriate way to safeguard financial interest is for the client to take control of the insurance issues. In doing so, clients, their lenders and investors will take comfort in knowing that if there is subsequent contamination, any claim will be paid direct to him without the onus of proving liability against others. An appropriately arranged insurance programme can remove many of the uncertainties from the site and promote further investment and development.

■ *consultants' and contractors' professional indemnity insurance*

The purpose of consultants' and contractors' professional indemnity insurance is often widely misunderstood by clients. It is not a benefit to the client. It is a defence mechanism, which will often be used by the insured and insurer to resist a claim against them. The onus is on clients to prove negligence against the consultant or contractor, and that can be a tortuous route with no guarantee of recovery. Even when negligence is ultimately proven, it can take years to gain compensation through the courts, with all the associated financial implications that can ensue.

Many consultants' and contractors' professional indemnity policies carry limitations, restrictions and exclusions that may prove unacceptable. Depending upon the policy, if the consultant or contractor becomes insolvent, professional indemnity insurance may become void.

The type of insurance needed would reflect how the contractor is to be employed and on what terms. For example, it is not uncommon for contractors to be appointed to carry out a full design-and-build package of works, whereby the contractor may not be insured because of professional indemnity insurance restrictions. Pollution exclusion clauses may apply, for example.

- *contractors' public liability insurance*

Contractors involved with remediation often carry ineffective insurance protection. Limits of indemnity may be inadequate and exclusions for gradual pollution often apply. Such risk is often heightened during remediation. For example, a site may be contaminated yet not be classed as "contaminated land" under Part IIA. The remediation activities can themselves create a linkage that causes a problem – for example, by making a pathway for the contamination to migrate to a sensitive receptor.

Unless a view is taken on the overall interaction of construction, similar problems can occur on a remediated site, when construction contractors are involved. For example, groundwork or foundation activities, such as piling, can create pathways for the migration of contaminants. Care is needed to establish with construction contractors whether they have gradual pollution exclusions within their public liability policies. If so, other risk management measures may have to be considered.

Construction insurance is only one of a number of insurance mechanisms that need to be considered as part of the development process. This is discussed in Chapter 8.

Action points

→ Clients should review the basis of control of construction insurances.

→ Check contractor's public liability and professional indemnity policies, particularly where issues of design are concerned, when design-and-build contracts are being let.

→ Obtain advice from specialist insurance brokers.

▶ *incorporating design issues*

The key issues developed through the investigation and design phases need to be adequately embraced in documents supporting the procurement process. How and to what degree the elements are incorporated will depend upon the selected form of contract. Matters to be considered include:

- how the remediation strategy and the final development concepts are designed to interact
- clarifying how such consents/permits/licences as may be required are obtained
- bringing forward health and safety management criteria
- bringing forward environmental protection criteria
- bringing forward archaeological issues
- bringing forward ecological matters
- embracing sustainability issues:
  - management of materials – reuse/recycling
  - transport – traffic management
  - noise management and control.

Public-sector investment initiative. Procurement selection to achieve integrated project management with shared duties

A partnership comprising the development agency, local county borough council and landholder, had a common objective for a major reclamation scheme – to fuel sustainable economic regeneration in an area that had seen a significant decline in its older, traditional industries.

Situated on a former steelworks site, the remediation works were completed with contributions from ERDF funding the joint venture partners. The works provide 1 km of infrastructure, and have made available 136 acres of developable land. The procurement route chosen by the client team was one of target cost using the NEC ECC Option C form of contract.

Lessons learned

To deliver the best possible end-product, the share mechanism procurement route ensured an integrated project with shared duties, where project and team performance was measured and founded on the concept of value engineering. In addition to the goal of best value for money, the project organisation allowed for:

■ the whole of the site to be reclaimed providing flexibility for future needs

■ reduced uncertainty from ground conditions, so enabling inward investors to make decisions more readily

■ reduced the risk of residual "unforeseen ground conditions" to future developments

■ a quick start for developments.

Action point

→ Ensure design issues are taken forward into construction procurement documentation.

▶ *incorporating planning conditions*

The planning process is likely to result in conditions being imposed that define certain activities to be undertaken and their extent and standards. To ensure seamless links with implementation stages these aspects need to be taken into account. See also nature conservation below.

Action point

→ Ensure relevant planning conditions are reflected in contract obligations.

▶ *site co-ordination issues*

Examples of other co-ordinating factors that may need to be incorporated in procurement documents are:

■ provision for access for any existing occupants on portions of the land during the works

■ protection of existing services

■ access provisions to existing service routes to allow for possible emergency repairs.

▶ **setting obligations of contractors**

Amongst the potential obligations that may be required of contractors are:

■ *access to third parties to inspect the works*

Third parties (regulators, their consultees or those who may have an interest in the site, such as eventual site purchasers and their advisers) may have made demands for information through reports. As part of their regulatory functions, or for the purposes of property negotiation, third parties may also require access to sites to inspect the works. This may extend to requirements for third parties to have access to progress reports and aspects of site progress meetings.

■ *information to third parties*

At the procurement stage, requirements for information from contractors, either for third parties and/or project management purposes should be carried across into procurement documentation. These processes may also dovetail with requirements for third parties to have access to inspect the works. The supply and submission of as-built construction records (often involving staged submissions to reflect progress) should be resolved and set out as obligations with prospective contractors.

■ *information for management purposes*

In addition to the general submissions of information, eg method statements/progress reporting/quality control records, further information may need to be defined to facilitate the management of the contract. For example, if landfill tax exemptions are applicable where clients are undertaking applications, they will require data on materials disposal in order to administer this process.

▶ **nature conservation**

Chapter 6 deals with the possible requirements for dealing with impacts upon protected species. In preparing for construction procurement, clients need to consider:

■ co-ordination of processes to obtain licences and permissions
■ the need to provide for dust and water quality monitoring, and noise monitoring and control, especially in the breeding seasons
■ protective or relocation measures related to species protection
■ fulfilling obligations arising from an environmental impact assessment or planning
■ provisions to cover discovery of protected species during the progress of construction.

▶ **accommodating specialist contractors**

Site remediation may involve various specialist activities. Specialist contractors providing specific services, eg groundwater treatment may have to be included within the contract team to work in conjunction with the main contractor.

Depending upon the manner of contracting, it may be appropriate to ask main contractors what experience they possess of working alongside specialist contractors such as companies offering bio-remediation or *in-situ* remediation technologies or experienced groundwork contractors experienced in contaminated spoil haulage and disposal.

Enquiries should also be made with prospective contracting parties at the procurement stage to establish whether there are any grounds that preclude them working together.

> ## Action point
>
> → Confirm compatibility of the contract team.

▶ **waste management**

The implementation of the Landfill Directive [52] and the introduction of PPC permits for landfills and other waste management operations is leading to more stringent standards and a possible increase in the disposal costs of wastes from projects involving previously developed land. Some of the issues for waste management are set out below.

▪ *do any of the works require a waste management licence?*

In general, wastes created by the construction process do not require a licence so long as they are removed promptly from the site and no processing takes place. If wastes are stored on site the environmental agencies may require a licence to be obtained. There are, however, several waste licensing exemptions contained in the Waste Management Licensing Regulations 1994 [53] that may assist with a variety of building and reclamation operations, but these have to be registered with the appropriate environmental agency and extra time should be allowed for this.

> ## Action points
>
> → The programme should incorporate a realistic timetable to deal with these issues and for discussions with the environmental agencies.
>
> → Great care is required in deciding whether a particular material is a waste; the designation of a material as a waste has significant financial implications. Designation of material as a waste is likely to inhibit reuse and may trigger significant disposal costs. Specialist legal advice may well be required.

▪ *do any of the site remediation works require a waste management licence?*

The Environment Agency published guidance in 2001 [54] on the relationship between waste management licensing and remediation. Clients should seek advice from their consultants and environmental lawyers on issues arising from the guidance.

▪ *do any of the remediation processes require a mobile plant licence?*

The temporary use of mobile plant for such purposes, that is for less than 28 days, will not generally require planning consent, but long-term use should be part of planning obtained for the development. A mobile plant licence will be required from the relevant environmental agency for mobile waste management or treatment operations.

▪ *are any crushing or screening operations to take place on the site?*

It is common for concrete and other demolition material from former buildings or hardstanding to be reused on or off the development site. This is particularly common with previously developed sites and offers opportunities for embracing sustainability criteria in line with CPA [3]. The introduction of the aggregates tax [50] will create an incentive for clients to create secondary aggregate from any available materials.

If mobile plant is being used for the crushing operations, the plant should be authorised as a Part B process under Part I of the Environmental Protection Act 1990 in the name of the operator and by reference to his principal place of business. A permit under the Pollution Prevention and Control

Chapter 7

(England and Wales) Regulations 2000 [55] became a requirement from 1 April 2002 for new processes, and existing processes are deemed to have applied on that date. The permitting authority is the local authority.

Action point

→ Responsibility for checking the existence of such an authorisation and contractual provisions made as to the operation of such plant should be identified and, where appropriate, set out in construction procurement documents.

■ *waste movements*

Provision should be made in documents for the generation, retention and access to proper records of all waste movements on and off the site. Duty of care transfer notes will be needed for non-special wastes under the Environmental Protection (Duty of Care) Regulations 1991 [56] and combined special waste consignment notes for the movement of special wastes so as to comply with the Special Waste Regulations 1996 [57] as amended.

All wastes must be carried by a carrier registered as a waste carrier under the Control of Pollution (Amendment) Act 1989 [58] and the Controlled Waste (Registration of Carriers and Seizure of Vehicles) Regulations 1991 [59]. That such registrations are in place should be cross-checked by obtaining details from the environmental agencies. Regulation is being introduced to require producers of special waste to be registered with the appropriate environmental agency.

Action points

→ Cross-check waste carrier registrations with the environmental agencies.

→ Responsibility should be allocated for inspection of sites receiving wastes and for inspection of waste licences.

→ Duty of care waste transfer notes should be retained for a minimum of two years and parties should comply with record-keeping requirements of Special Waste Regulations (as amended).

▶ *landfill tax exemptions*

The preconditions relating to whether wastes qualify for the contaminated land exemption are set out in Section 6.3. Key issues at this stage are:

■ *application for exemptions.* Landowners, developers or main contractors can make the application. Care should be taken on notice periods

■ *disposal sites.* Disposal sites must be nominated.

The law provides for exemption from landfill tax for certain wastes arising from the reclamation of contaminated land. Sections 43a and 43b of the Finance Act 1996 [60] as inserted by Landfill Tax Contaminated Land (Order 1996), SI 1996 (1529) [61]. Under Landfill Tax Guidance Note 2 (LFT 2) [62], a reclamation will qualify for exemption if it falls within one of the following categories (provided that it also meets certain conditions):

(a) It is, or is to be, carried out with the objective of facilities and development, conservation, the provision of a public path or other amenity, or the use of a landfill agricultural or forestry.

(b) In the case of others than within paragraph (a) above, it is, or is to be, carried out with the object of reducing or removing the potential pollutants to cause harm.

Pollutants do not necessarily need to be cleared from the land to qualify for the exemption, but the cause of the pollution must have ceased. In addition, the land must not be subject to a works or a remediation notice served under the Water Resources Act 1991 (49) or Part IIA of the Environmental Protection Act 1990 [7] respectively.

Other exemptions relate to dredgings and mining and quarrying wastes, and clients should take specialist advice as to whether these are applicable.

> ## Action points
>
> → Establish who is to make the application for landfill tax exemption.
> → Application for exemption must be made to Customs and Excise in advance of removal of wastes and the parties should be clear who has this responsibility.
> → Clients and advisers should refer to Customs and Excise Note LFT 2 *Reclamation of contaminated land* (May 2001) for further guidance [62].

▶ *water pollution*

The parties should clarify who is responsible for obtaining discharge consents or abstraction licences that may be required for the development. In particular, there is often misunderstanding over the disposal of water from the works into local watercourses. Draining over grassed or wooded areas and then into a watercourse is only acceptable if formally agreed with the Environment Agency. The Environment Agency is concerned at the impact of suspended solids on watercourses and views the construction industry as a major polluter of water. Formal discharge arrangements are likely to be required.

> ## Action point
>
> → The cost and time for dealing with water pollution matters must be realistically appraised.

▶ *health and safety*

Health and safety provisions need to be integrated for the particular remediation processes to be applied to the site. See Section 7.3 below.

▶ *data management – developing the site log*

Utilising the site log as a source document for overall scheme design was described in Chapter 6. Much of the activity at this procurement stage will be supplying information to prospective contractors. Maintaining the site log at this stage to cover records of related activities and exchanges of information with contractors will permit the log to be the primary repository of project information.

> ## Action point
>
> → Maintain entries into the site log.

7.3 KEY ISSUES FOR CONSTRUCTION PROCUREMENT: IMPLEMENTATION

As with all construction matters, the implementation stages will benefit from the preparation and attention applied to procurement documentation. The history and past uses of previously developed sites are often complex, so it is quite likely that during construction matters will be encountered that were not foreseen in the design stages. These issues need to be managed as and when they occur. The project team needs to be able to demonstrate flexibility and an ability to act and respond quickly to situations, coupled with measured and effective communication skills.

▶ **reviewing advisers**

Depending on the nature of the procurement process, advisers' competencies should be reviewed to establish their relevance to the construction stage.

▶ **is the selected remediation strategy compatible with development planning and design?**

The inherent variability of ground conditions means that construction often encounters circumstances that were not incorporated in the design stage. This has implications for the detailed dovetailing of remediation work into the design of the final development. Preparatory work undertaken within the design stages can cater for such eventualities by incorporating flexibility into construction project programming and site designs. Nevertheless, it is important to maintain a watching brief during the construction stages to ensure that the overall development package remains viable.

Figure 7.2 *Example of site clearance*

▶ **verification**

Monitoring and supervision of quality control will be required to reinforce provisions for the verification stage. Effective communication will also be important.

▶ **waste**

Waste management issues are considered in Section 7.2. Implications at this implementation stage need to be taken into account.

▶ **health and safety**

Site activities should be conducted with an awareness of the management of interrelated health and safety matters that apply to the development process. Similarly, the developing health and safety plan at construction stage will cover all aspects of the site relating to both development and remediation. Close attention may be needed on the interfaces between remediation works and building and site construction, to ensure that the management of the development as a whole is effective.

▶ **environmental protection**

CIRIA's guide [42] provides advice on the application of good practice principles.

▶ **consents/permits/licences**

For details on possible permissions, refer to Appendix 7.

▶ **embracing sustainable development criteria**

The provisions developed in design stages and carried forward into the procurement documents can now be put into practice.

▶ **communication with planners/consultees/regulators**

Provisions for maintaining dialogues need to be maintained.

▶ **communications and consultations with third parties**

Communications with third parties will have been planned during previous design and procurement stages. This process needs to be brought into action during construction. If not already formed, it may be advisable to establish a formal liaison group incorporating local residents and other interest groups.

▶ **landfill tax exemptions**

There will be continuing requirements for more information.

▶ **data management – the site log**

Continuing the site log through the implementation stage will result in an updated site reference document that can be used at subsequent stages of the development process (see Chapter 8). Further information on content of the site log is contained in Appendix 11.

▶ **reports**

Refer to Appendix 11 for range of reports at this implementation of construction stage.

7.4 KEY GUIDANCE

7.4.1 General

Department of Environment, Food and Rural Affairs

> (In prep) and Environment Agency CLR11 *Handbook of model procedures for the management of contaminated land – Overview*

> (In prep) and Environment Agency CLR 11 *Handbook of model procedures for the management of contaminated land – MP 3 Implementation of risk management measures*

Scotland and Northern Ireland Forum for Environmental Research (SNIFFER)

> (1999) Project Number SR97(11)F. *Communicating understanding of contaminated land risks*

Scottish Environment Protection Agency (SEPA) and Environment Agency

> Pollution Prevention Guidance Notes (PPG(**))

> (1999) PPG 5 *Works in, near or liable to affect watercourses*

> (1998) PPG 6 *Working at construction and demolition sites*

Health and Safety Executive

> (1991) HS (G) 66 *Protection of workers and the general public during development of contaminated land*

Construction Industry Research and Information Association

> (1999) Report C502. Coventry, S and Woolveridge, C *Environmental good practice on site*

7.4.2 Construction procurement

Environment Agency

(2001) *Guidance on the application of waste management licensing to remediation*, Version 2.0

(2001) *Mobile plant and contaminated soil remediation: an overview*

(2001) *Guidance on the disposal of contaminated soils*, Version 3

(In prep) Project P5-046. *Supporting guidance for the verification of risk assessment and risk management measures*

7.4.3 Construction implementation

Environment Agency

(2001) *Mobile plant and contaminated soil remediation: an overview*

(2001) *Guidance on the disposal of contaminated soils*, Version 3

Construction Industry Research and Information Association

(1995) SP102 *Remedial treatment for contaminated land. Vol II Decommissioning, decontamination and demolition*

(1995) SP105 *Remedial treatment for contaminated land. Vol V Excavation and disposal*

(1996) R132 Steeds, J E, Shepherd, E and Barry, D L *A guide for safe working practices on contaminated sites*

(1997) R133 Guthrie, P, Woolveridge, A, Patel, C *Waste minimisation in construction – a site guide*

Chapter 8

Completion of the development objectives

When the project is complete it is important to measure whether the objectives that were set at the outset have been met, not just in physical, but also in financial, terms. This could mean different things to different clients, but the objective may well be to profit from the development of previously developed land or occupy it as owner-occupier, or to take a lease.

Recurring themes have been presented during the preceding chapters that dealt with the key stages of the development cycle. These issues are material to the completion of the process.

Figure 5.1 illustrates the various stages and interactions likely to come about in the development process. Ultimately the process finishes with completion of the development and the objectives of the original feasibility appraisal being met in financial terms. This is the acid test of the development cycle as to whether the project has been a success.

This chapter identifies the key issues that enable the project to reach a successful conclusion. It sets out the steps that need to be taken to conclude the development cycle.

Key issues covered in Chapter 8

- financial review
- consents/permits/licences
- data management – the site log
- warranties
- health and safety
- planning conditions
- environmental protection
- land condition records/land quality statements

- indemnities
- insurance
- data management – as-built drawings
- reports
- appointment of appropriate marketing consultants
- leasehold transactions

8.1 POLICY AND PROFESSIONAL ISSUES

Although dealt with earlier in this guide, certain policy and professional matters need to be discussed here. They are essential parts of the transaction process, given their impact on professional obligations, particularly upon solicitors. These are listed below.

▶ **Part IIA exclusion tests and agreements on liabilities**

The statutory guidance to implement Part IIA of the Environmental Protection Act 1990 identifies exclusion tests whereby an appropriate person is excluded from the class of persons liable under the Act. These are discussed in respect of risk transfer in Chapter 3.

▶ **The Law Society's warning card**

In June 2001, the Law Society published its warning card [28], which requires solicitors in every case where property or land is being bought or sold to advise clients to consider whether contamination is an issue. Implications are discussed in Chapter 4 and its content is reproduced in Appendix 13.

8.2 KEY ISSUES

If the issues set out in the preceding chapters of this guidance have been addressed, a structure should have been established to allow the measurement of the financial and physical performance during the life of the project.

▶ *financial review*

Cost will have been a central issue through the development of the site. The performance of the project will have required careful cost control during the development life cycle. The timing of sales and lettings depends upon macro-economic cycles as much as local issues, both of which cannot be predicted. However, the development must maintain financial discipline and once the cashflow cycle has been completed the initial rate of return needs to be equal to or better than that predicted at the outset.

Action points

➔ Ensure that all grant monies have been drawn down at the key points in the cashflow.

➔ Ensure that the landfill tax exemptions have been fully accounted for.

➔ If the site is contaminated and tax relief is necessary as part of the corporation tax payments made by the company, it is important that a separate assessment of the qualifying expenditure has been made for the companies' tax return.

▶ *consents/permits/licences*

When the property is being made available for sale, access to the site by purchasers, lessees and their professional advisers may be necessary. Appendix 7 deals with third-party approvals at this stage.

Action point

➔ Ensure that notice is given before entry and that a health and safety record of visitors is maintained.

▶ *data management – the site log*

The benefits in collecting and managing data via a site log were highlighted in Chapter 3. These become apparent at the point of sale.

A carefully prepared package of information made available to the purchaser when the property is being sold or let in the open market has great advantages. It can be time-consuming and costly to assemble the information during the conveyancing process, so it is essential that data management continues through the predevelopment, construction and post-completion phases.

Sellers of land take care that the information they provide is accurate and must avoid misrepresentation of the condition of the land or property, because of the Property Misdescriptions Act 1991 [63]. In addition, as noted in *A changing landscape: the valuation of contaminated land and property* [64], if the buyer or lessee is given information that is difficult to interpret or understand it may jeopardise the sale.

> **Action points**
>
> → Ensure that responsibility for the collation of the data is allocated to an individual.
> → Ensure that the data is presented in a form which is user-friendly to all parties.
> → Ensure that the data is presented in a consistent format.

▶ *warranties*

Various professional teams are involved in the development of previously developed land. Those engaged in the design and construction processes, including both above-ground and below-ground issues, must provide a warranty to underpin their advice and activities. The warranty forms part of the original appointment documentation highlighted in Chapter 3.

> **Action points**
>
> → The warranties, which form part of the appointment packages, must be completed before the development has been finished.
> → The specialist legal advisers must co-ordinate and collate the warranties and appointment data.

▶ *health and safety*

When finished, the development will be accompanied by a health and safety file, and the related documentation to implement this must be made available at the point of sale or letting. There is a continuing obligation on the client to keep this file up to date.

> **Action point**
>
> → The health and safety file must be compiled in accordance with the requirements of the CDM Regulations.

▶ *planning conditions*

Chapter 5 highlighted the need to include the requirements of planning conditions within designs. The planning conditions may involve continuing obligations, such as gas, water and air monitoring of the land, as well as the building services. It may also include restrictions on, for example, hours of working and traffic movement.

The development cannot be considered complete until the local planning authority has agreed that all the planning obligations have been met.

> **Action points**
>
> → Ensure that planning conditions are reflected in the contract obligations.
> → Obtain confirmation from the local planning authority that planning conditions have been complied with.

Chapter 8

▶ **environmental protection**

In sensitive areas of nature conservation, and perhaps where the property is situated in an area of outstanding natural beauty or a conservation area, the occupier of the completed development may have to meet ongoing obligations, such as longer-term monitoring of remediation.

> **Action point**
>
> → Ensure that third parties meet obligations for environmental protection.

▶ **land condition records/land quality statements**

The statutory environmental bodies are unlikely to give an unqualified statement that the land has been cleaned of contaminants to allow the development to be successfully completed. The professional team, particularly the SiLC and the chartered environmental surveyor, therefore need to ascertain whether the issues identified at the outset were dealt with during the construction stage. It is important to establish that the land is no longer contaminated land within the meaning of Section 78A(2) of Part IIA of the Environmental Protection Act 1990 [7].

Development of the land condition record is discussed in Chapter 3. It also covers the purpose of the land quality statement, which effectively forms the close-out report for the project.

> **Action points**
>
> → Ensure all documents material to the identification and remediation of contaminated land form part of the land quality statement.
>
> → The land condition record (LCR) should be prepared by a qualified specialist in land condition (SiLC) or appropriately qualified.
>
> → Land quality statements should be prepared by a chartered environmental surveyor.

▶ **indemnities**

Quite often either the vendor or the purchaser requires a financial indemnity for losses, particularly where it involves contaminated land. Much hinges upon the financial well-being of both parties for the long term since many of these indemnities are in perpetuity. While they provide a degree of comfort, they are not a certain method of conveying risk at the closure of the development cycle.

> **Action point**
>
> → If indemnities are to be granted it is important to ensure that they are backed up by company guarantees and that they can be relied upon by third parties in the longer term.

▶ **insurance**

Although the land may have been comprehensively remediated in accordance with the requirements of the planning authority and the environmental agencies, the remedial technologies employed may leave some uncertainties for the longer term. The design team and contractors involved with the project will have professional indemnity insurance and will have entered into warranties, as discussed in Chapter 7, but the level of protection they provide is limited, particularly where complex remediation and construction has taken place. Furthermore, clients are reliant upon their advisers remaining in business in the longer term and adequate professional indemnity insurance being maintained.

Reliance has commonly been placed on the professional indemnity insurance of the consultants, backed up by warranties, but these cover a relatively short time-span in comparison with the life of the property. For example, a warranty under seal will provide 12 years of assurance, whereas the building obsolescence may exceed 50 years.

Several insurance policies may be purchased for newly built structures. Latent defects, title insurance, and buildings insurance for contents as well as for damage to the structure are required in addition to contractors' public liability policies and other special insurances. These are normally addressed during the construction and post-construction phases, particularly at the point of sale.

From the client's perspective, the most appropriate way to safeguard financial interest is to take control of the insurance issues. By doing so, clients, their lenders and investors know that if contamination is discovered subsequently, any claim will be paid direct to the client without the onus of proving liability against others. An appropriately arranged insurance programme can remove many of the uncertainties from the site and promote further investment and development. Different insurance products relating to environmental matters are summarised in Table 8.1 below. These should be considered in conjunction with title insurance, latent defects, all risk property, business interruption and loss of profit insurance.

Table 8.1   *Insurance packages*

Form of insurance	Coverage
Stop loss	Cost overrun or unforeseen circumstances during decontamination works
First- and third-party environmental	First- and third-party cover for contamination-related claims or remediation costs
Tenant covenant	Tenant covenant – inability to service rent due under lease
Mortgage indemnity	Contamination-related incident leading to inability to service loan or to repay borrowing
Business interruption	Business interruption costs and losses to tenant arising from contamination-related incident requiring remediation
Loss of profit	Loss of rent and other associated costs arising from a contamination-related claim

Action points

→   Take advice from a specialist environmental insurance broker.

→   Before disposal of the completed development, consider obtaining an indication of insurance terms with draft policy wording before the property is placed on the market.

→   If not employed to date, consider insurance if contamination is an issue of contention.

▶   *data management – as-built drawings*

As part of the data management process and as highlighted in previous chapters, a package of as-built drawings, including services information that forms part of the site log, must be freely available. In terms of obligations for health and safety, clients need to ensure as-built drawings are included in the health and safety file.

Chapter 8

> **Action point**
>
> → Ensure that as-built drawings are made available to the appointed person in the legal team before marketing.

▶ *reports*

Refer to Appendix 11 for range of relevant reports at completion stage.

▶ *appointment of appropriate marketing consultants*

During the life of the project the client should have appointed a professional surveying team to provide market advice for the project. It may be necessary to appoint marketing agents, to act both as a professional property agency and for public relations purposes, to deal with the letting and/or the sale phase.

The consultant will require assurance that the data for the components of the sale are available both to support the marketing initiatives and to ensure that the Property Misdescriptions Act is not contravened.

> **Action points**
>
> → The marketing team is an integral part of the design process and should be appointed early in the cycle.
>
> → The appointment should be incentive-led.
>
> → A well-defined budget and cashflow should be established at the outset, together with an efficient marketing campaign.

▶ *leasehold transactions*

While properties may ultimately be sold as investments or to owner-occupiers, many of them are let on leases from which an income stream is generated and value created. The leaseholder needs to be aware of the issues just as much as other parties involved with the development process or where a freehold sale is contemplated. The lease between the parties determines the quality of the landlord–tenant relationship.

Issues to be addressed before the grant of a lease of a previously developed property include the following.

1 Who is to be responsible for liabilities arising from past contamination that was present on the site at the date of the lease that may have come from third-party sites?

2 Does the site require monitoring in the longer term? Apportioning the costs between the landlord and the tenant must be transparent at the time the lease is entered into. The lease must also specify who is responsible for discharging any continuing obligations.

3 Detailed consideration should be given to the wording of leasehold covenants and the impact that contamination may have on such items as conveyance and repair, rent review, insurance, nuisance prevention, compliance with statutes, payment of outgoings, yielding up, service charge provisions.

4 Should a schedule of environmental condition be prepared to highlight the fact that the condition of the land at the time that the lease is granted will not have materially altered unless the tenant causes contamination to occur and the assets to depreciate?

8.3 KEY GUIDANCE

RICS Books

(2000) *Contamination and its implications for chartered surveyors*

The College of Estate Management

(2001) *The contaminated land regime: impacts of the property industry and estate management issues*

(1995) *A changing landscape: the valuation of contaminated land and property*

Law Society

(2001) *Contaminated land – the warning card*

Urban Task Force Working Group

(2000) *A standard land condition record*, prepared by a working group of the Urban Task Force

References

1   DETR (Department of the Environment, Transport and the Regions) (2000). Planning Policy Guidance Note 3 – *Housing*. Stationery Office, London.

2   DETR (Department of the Environment, Transport and the Regions) (1996). *Household growth: where shall we live? A Green Paper.* Stationery Office, London.

3   RICS/Environment Agency (2000). *Comprehensive project appraisal – towards sustainability.* RICS, London.

4   Syms, P M (2001). *Releasing brownfields, a research report on behalf of Joseph Rowntree Foundation.* RICS Foundation, April 2000.

5   Urban Task Force (1999). *Towards an urban renaissance. Final report of the UTF.* E and FN Spon, London.

6   RICS (1998). *Accessing private finance: the availability and effectiveness of private finance in urban regeneration.* University of Ulster.

7   Environmental Protection Act (EPA) 1990.

8   Environment Act 1995.

9   DETR (Department of the Environment, Transport and the Regions) (2000). *Environmental Protection Act 1990: Part IIA Contaminated Land Circular 02/2000.* DETR, London.

10   Department for Transport Local Government and the Regions (2002). *Draft Technical Advice Note: Development on land affected by contamination, a Planning Policy Guidance Note.* Stationery Office, London.

11   (In prep). *Draft Environment Agency internal guidance on planning application responses relating to land contamination, Part IIA and the planning regime.*

12   Finnamore, J, Denton, B and Nathanail, C P (2000). *Land contamination – management of financial risk.* CIRIA, London.

13   DEFRA and Environment Agency (in prep). CLR 11 *Handbook of model procedures for the management of contaminated land – overview.*

14   DEFRA and Environment Agency (in prep). CLR 11 *Handbook of model procedures for the management of contaminated land – MP 1 Site assessment.*

15   DEFRA and Environment Agency (in prep). CLR 11 *Handbook of model procedures for the management of contaminated land – MP 2 Selection and evaluation of remedial measures.*

16   DEFRA and Environment Agency (in prep). CLR 11 *Handbook of model procedures for the management of contaminated land – MP 3 Implementation of risk management measures.*

17   DETR (2000). *Our towns and cities: the future. Delivering an urban renaissance, the Urban White Paper, 2000.* Stationery Office, London.

18   DETR (2000). *By design – urban design in the planning system: towards better practice.* Thomas Telford, London.

19   DETR (2000). *Building a better quality of life – a strategy for more sustainable construction.* Stationery Office, London.

20   Llewelyn-Davies (2000). *Urban Design Compendium.* English Partnerships and the Housing Corporation.

21   Environment Agency and NHBC (2000). *Guidance for the safe development of housing on land affected by contamination.* R and D Publication 66.

22   Health and Safety at Work etc Act 1974.

23   Construction (Design and Management) Regulations 1994 (as amended).

24   Urban Task Force Working Group (2000). *A standard land condition record.* Prepared by a working group of the Urban Task Force.

25   RICS (2000). *Contamination and its implications for chartered surveyors.* RICS Books, March 2000.

26   DTLR/RICS. Guidance note. *Brownfield Improvement Grant (BIG): partnership support for land and property regeneration schemes: direct development, speculative development, non-speculative (bespoke) development.*

27   Finance Act 2001.

28   Law Society (2001). *Contaminated land – the warning card.* Law Society, London.

29   British Standards Institution (2001). BS 10175:2001, *Code of practice for the investigation of potentially contaminated sites.* BSi London.

30   Environment Agency (2000). R and D Project P5-065/TR, *Technical aspects of site investigation,* Vols 1 and 2. Environment Agency, Bristol.

31   Welsh Development Agency (1993). *WDA manual on the remediation of contaminated land.* WDA, Cardiff.

32   Scotland and Northern Ireland Forum for Environmental Research (1999). Project Number SR 97 (11) F, *Communicating understanding of contaminated land risks.*

33   DoE (1994). PPG 23, *Planning and pollution control, a Planning Policy Guidance Note.* Stationery Office, London.

34   DoE (1995). DoE Circular 11/95, *The use of conditions in planning permissions.* Stationery Office, London.

35   DTLR (2001). The Planning Green Paper. *Planning: delivering a fundamental change.* Stationery Office, London.

36   DoE (1997). DOE Circular 1/97, *Planning obligations.* Stationery Office, London.

37   CIC Construction Guide (in prep). *Brownfields: building on previously developed land: a briefing guide for construction clients.*

38   The Town and Country (Environmental Impact Assessment) (England and Wales) Regulations 1999.

39   Wildlife and Countryside Act 1981 (as amended). The Conservation (Natural Habitats etc) Regulations 1994.

40   DETR (2000). Planning Policy Guidance Note 9, *Nature conservation*. Stationery Office, London.

41   AGS (2000). *Guidelines for combined geoenvironmental and geotechnical investigation*.

42   Coventry, S and Woolveridge, C (1999). Publication C502, *Environmental good practice on site*. CIRIA, London.

43   Environment Agency (in prep). *Monitoring Certification Scheme (MCERTS) to the chemical testing of soils*.

44   The Management of Health and Safety at Work Regulations 1999.

45   The Control of Substances Hazardous to Health Regulations (COSHH) 1999.

46   The Construction (Health Safety and Welfare) Regulations 1996.

47   The Management and Administration of Safety and Health at Mines Regulations 1993.

48   Mines and Quarries (Tips) Act 1969.

49   The Water Resources Act 1991.

50   Mines and Quarries Act 1954.

51   Environment Agency (in prep). Project P5-046, *Supporting guidance for the verification of risk assessment and risk management measures*.

52   Landfill Directive 1999/31/EC.

53   Waste Management Licensing Regulations 1994.

54   Environment Agency (2001). *Guidance on the application of waste management licensing to remediation*, Version 2.0.

55   Pollution Prevention and Control (England and Wales) Regulations 2000.

56   Environmental Protection (Duty of Care) Regulations 1991.

57   The Special Waste Regulations 1996 (as amended).

58   Control of Pollution (Amendment) Act 1989.

59   The Controlled Waste (Registration of Carriers and Seizure of Vehicles) Regulations 1991.

60   The Finance Act 2001 – the aggregates levy (Clauses 16–49 and Schedules 4–10).

61   Landfill Tax Contaminated Land Order 1996 (SI 1996 (1529)).

62   Customs and Excise Note LFT 2. *Reclamation of contaminated land*. May 2001.

63   The Property Misdescriptions Act 1991.

64   The College of Estate Management (1995). *A changing landscape: the valuation of contaminated land and property*.

65   DoE (1995). *Our future homes: opportunity choice responsibility. The government's housing policies for England and Wales*. Stationery Office, London.

66   DoE (1995). *Projections of households in England 2016*. Stationery Office, London.

67   Laidler, D W, Bryce, A J and Boswell, J (unpublished). *Guidance on the sale and transfer of land which may be affected by contamination*. CIRIA, London.

68   DoE (1995). *Household growth: where shall we live?* Stationery Office, London.

69   Brehen and Hall (1996). *Enquiry into housing need and provision*. Town and Country Planning Association.

70   Kass, G A (1998). *A brown and pleasant land: household growth and brownfield sites*. Parliamentary Office of Science and Technology (POST), House of Commons, 1998. London.

71   DoE (1997). CLR 12, *A quality approach for contaminated land consultancy*. DoE, London.

72   Construction (Design and Management) Regulations 1994 (2001). *Managing health and safety in construction, approved code of practice*.

73   Environment Agency. *Environment Agency policy and guidelines on the use of anti-pollution works notices*.

74   Healey, P *et al* (ed) (1992). *Rebuilding the city – property-led urban regeneration*. E & FN Spon.

75   Townsend, M (2001). "Contaminated land regime – warning to all". *Law Society Gazette*, 29 October 2001.

Appendix 1 Brownfield sites – policy and commercial drivers

This appendix examines the policy and commercial drivers for developing previously developed land and why this has come about. The term "brownfield" has been applied to reflect its usage in the Parliamentary Office of Science and Technology (POST) report [71] referred to in the text.

A1.1 THE BROWNFIELD DYNAMIC

A1.1.1 Government policy development

In response to the demand for additional housing, the government has generated initiatives aimed at fulfilling its target of 60 per cent of new housing being built on brownfield rather than greenfield sites. These initiatives include:

- commissioning of the Urban Task Force report *Towards an urban renaissance* [5]
- the resulting government Urban White Paper, *Towns and cities: the future – delivering an urban renaissance*, November 2000 [17]
- DETR Circular 02/2000, *Contaminated land* [9]
- publication of the Planning Policy Guidance Note PPG 3, *Housing* in March 2000 [1]
- *The government's housing policies for England and Wales in 1995: our future homes – opportunity, choice, responsibility* [65]
- *Projections of households in England 2016*, Department of Environment,1995 [66]
- *Household growth: where shall we live?* Department of the Environment, 1996 [67].

> *The Government is committed to maximising the re-use of previously developed land and empty properties and the conversion of non-residential buildings for housing, in order both to promote regeneration and minimise the amount of Greenfield land being taken for development.*
>
> PPG 3, *Housing*, Paragraph 22 [1]

The 1995 Housing White Paper [68], a formal review of housing issues and policy, included a brief statement that 50 per cent of all new residential dwellings should be built on reused urban land by 2005. The target prompted several questions: could it be achieved; was it too tough; was it too soft; what benefits and what losses would ensue?

The debate was carried out in parallel with discussions on the consequences of the growth in the numbers of households. The major proposal was to raise the 50 per cent threshold to 60 per cent. However, the Town and Country Planning Association's *Enquiry into housing need and provision* [69] found that professionals believed that, without significant government policy changes, the proportion of houses being built on used urban sites was unlikely to exceed 40 per cent. The Urban Task Force Report *Towards an urban renaissance* [5] also concluded that, without significant policy shifts, there was little likelihood of accommodating 60 per cent of new dwellings on previously developed land.

The government responded by implementing a policy review. This resulted in Planning Policy Guidance Note 3, published in March 2000 [1] and the Urban White Paper, *Towns and cities: the future – delivering an urban renaissance*, published in November 2000 [17].

The Council for the Protection of Rural England (CPRE) estimated in March 2001 that the initiatives were being thwarted because greenfield land is available for 658 000 houses, which is sufficient to accommodate the demands of the largest 80 house-builders for six years before they need to touch an urban site. It also noted that government regional offices had approved the development of 15 000 houses on 671 hectares of rural land.

Parliament has acknowledged that persuading developers to use brownfield sites instead of greenfield locations is proving difficult. It is particularly true where opportunities exist for development on land that has not been used before or where greenfield sites can be purchased easily. In greenfield locations there are no site assembly issues and extensive remedial works are rarely necessary, although infrastructure costs can be higher.

In 1998 the Parliamentary Office of Science and Technology (POST) published *A brown and pleasant land: household growth and brownfield sites* [70], which sought to encapsulate the development frictions that can undermine government policies and the opportunities presented by brownfield sites.

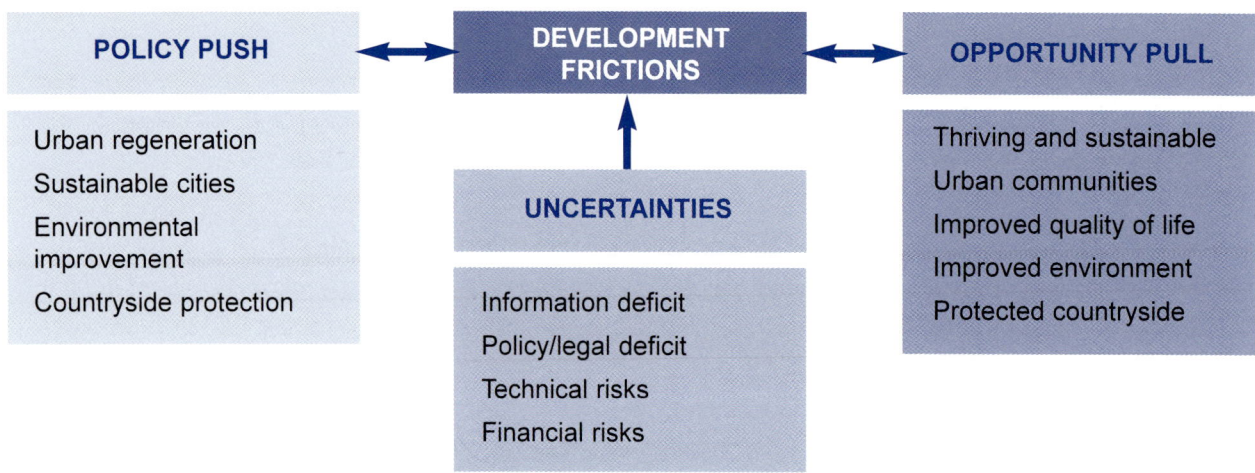

Figure A1.1   *The brownfield dynamic* [70]

> *The Opportunity Pull drives the Policy Push and the desire to provide the homes required (eg to tackle urban deprivation, poor environmental quality and to protect the countryside). At the same time, however, uncertainties create Development Frictions that work against both the Policy Push and the Opportunity Pull.*
>
> *For example there may be technical problems associated with financial institutions and prospective owners or tenants may be reluctant to take on the risks involved. Furthermore, a lack of information on the availability and viability of Brownfield land for redevelopment means that developers find it difficult to plan their housing projects into the long term.*
>
> *Moreover, a lack of a comprehensive and clear legal framework, and sets of procedures and standards for tackling sites (again, contaminated land is a key problem here), also leads to confusion and variable (and possibly conflicting) approaches by different regulatory agencies, although the Environment Agency is working with the local authorities to overcome this.*

Source: POST publication
A brown and pleasant land: household growth and brownfield sites [70]

POST referred to contaminated land as a key issue in its deliberations.

Since the report was published, the government has implemented the Part IIA regime with Circular 02/2000. The regime came into force in England on 1 April 2000, and in Scotland and Wales in July 2000 and July 2001. From a practical viewpoint, however, a hiatus then occurred. Initially, each local authority had to prepare a formal inspection strategy to identify land in its area that might be contaminated. Fifteen months was allowed for the drafting, consultation and publication of the authorities' strategies.

A1.1.2 Brownfield development – is it driven by supply or is it opportunity-led?

Development projects are key to the transformation of urban environments. Derelict, run-down former industrial areas, waterfront locations, and the declining, neglected, historical parts of towns and city centres have been targeted for new patterns of land use, often backed by substantial incentive packages. Such schemes can attract inward investment by providing appropriate accommodation and environments for new sectors of the economy. Landowners try to realise the capital value of their assets through the increasing site values that are attached to new development activities. The development process is driven by a combination of forces interacting with each other. Table A1.1 illustrates the interactions as a series of models and driving forces.

Table A1.1   *The driving forces of the development industry and the development of urban regeneration*

Model	Driving force
Supply-side constraints	Underlying consumer demand
Landowning capital and rent	"Landowners" search to safeguard rates of return on land and property investment
Institutional relations	Competition between local interests and national and international financial and property interests
Financial crises and economic restructuring	(a) Flows of finance capital on a national/ international scale (b) Spatial restructuring for economic restructuring

Consumer demand often constrains the development process unless real economic growth is achieved. In fragile economies with depressed property markets, market demand has to be created and maintained. Local authorities or public-sector agencies frequently have to use their powers to stimulate development activities. In areas of regeneration, the competition between local, national and international financial and property interests for control over development and investment opportunities leads to a national increase in confidence.

Economic restructuring in certain areas, particularly those with disadvantaged economies, also creates a driving force in brownfield developments. Research into these driving forces from 1992 [74] looked at various regeneration projects and brownfield developments, and acknowledged that they are constrained by:

- planning policies
- highway proposals
- landownership
- competition
- topographical or environmental features.

A fundamental constraint to development of previously developed land is site acquisition. Planning authorities have to ensure there is a supply of land for development in their areas. For developers, brownfield development is likely to be opportunity-led, as land and buildings come on to the market in the context of the local authority's planning policies. The attractiveness of a development is likely to result more from its location and its availability for acquisition, which needs to outrank other constraining factors.

Occupiers are also driven by opportunity, although they run to a markedly different agenda. For commercial occupiers, the opportunity may be driven by the need to fulfil a business objective of obtaining a market share for their products in a given area where the inhibiting factors are supplies and site constraints.

Development occurs because of the:

- market need
- availability of land
- economic and the business objectives of the occupier.

For developers, the main criterion is the ease with which they can achieve their selected development strategy. They will look at completing their development strategy as the process of maximising opportunity.

The developer is not necessarily the investor and is often the facilitator. In turn, therefore, an investor may be a person or a fund that acquires the completed property to fulfil financial goals. Commercial property is acquired to generate an income stream and to accumulate capital. Residential properties are acquired for occupancy, but the homeowner also hopes to enjoy capital growth. The developer must ensure that there is a market both for occupancy and for the investment once the project has been completed.

To complete the strategy successfully, the development process is often achieved through the line of least resistance. Brownfield issues and the complexity surrounding them can lead to this being compromised.

The importance of achieving completion of such a strategy was emphasised in the CIRIA publication *Land contamination – management of financial risk*[12].

This publication highlights the importance of the development of an appropriate sales strategy to enable the developer to exit successfully from the cycle of the development. It includes the following steps.

1   Provide full documentation of any remediation or site investigations in the conveyance records. This will increase the possibility that the prospective purchaser will fall into the Class A persons category under the Part IIA regime. The records may also form the basis of an exclusion from liability for contamination caused by future owners and occupiers.

2   Subject to negotiations, avoid where possible providing warranties (especially those relating to fitness for purpose (and indemnities to purchasers)).

3   Seek, where possible, indemnities that clearly assign to the purchaser the responsibility for new contamination arising after completion.

4   Finance potential losses by building up funds beforehand, or paying for losses retrospectively. Alternatively, contingent liabilities may be financed externally through specialist insurance.

A1.1.3 Further reading

Department of the Environment, Transport and the Regions (1998). *Planning for sustainable development: towards better practice*. Stationery Office, London.

Department of the Environment, Transport and the Regions (1991). *Policy appraisal and the environment: a guide for government departments*. Stationery Office, London.

DCMS (2000). *Better public buildings*.

Syms, P M (1994). The funding of developments on derelict and contaminated sites, in Ball, R and Pratt, A C, *Industrial property policy and economic development* Routledge, London, pp 63–82.

Syms, P and Knight, P (2000). *Building homes on used land*. RICS Books, London.

Syms, P (2002). *Land, development and design*. Blackwell Publishing, Oxford.

Appendix 2 Statutory provisions on contaminated land

A2.1 DEFINING CONTAMINATED LAND UNDER PART IIA OF THE ENVIRONMENTAL PROTECTION ACT 1990

The statutory provisions contained in Part IIA of the Environmental Protection Act (EPA) 1990 (Part IIA)[7], and inserted into the EPA by Section 57 of the Environment Act 1995[8], came into force on 1 April 2000 in England. They were implemented subsequently in Scotland and Wales in July 2000 and July 2001, respectively.

For England, the statutory provisions should be read in conjunction with DETR Circular 02/2000[9], which incorporated statutory guidance provisions under the Act. These were implemented by the Contaminated Land (England) Regulations 2000, SI 2000/227.

Separate statutory guidance provisions have been made for Scotland and Wales – see Appendix 12.

To date, provisions for Northern Ireland have not been implemented.

Part IIA provides a statutory definition of land that is contaminated. This definition is devised for application to the particular legislative regime of Part IIA and relates to the specific duties of local authorities to regulate land within their areas.

> *"Contaminated land" is defined at Section 78A(2) as:*
>
> *"any land which appears to the local authority whose area it is situated to be in such a condition by reasons of substances, in on or under the land, that:*
>
> *(a) significant harm is being caused or there is a significant possibility of such harm being caused, or;*
> *(b) pollution of controlled waters is being, or likely to be caused"*

The intended role of the Part IIA regime is to provide:

> *an improved system for the identification and remediation of land where contamination is causing unacceptable risks to human health or the wider environment, assessed in the context of the current use and circumstances of the land[9].*

The main point is that the regime deals with the current or existing use of land. For future land use, development is being considered under the planning regime.

The government's wider approach to contaminated land in the context of future land use and development is covered in Chapter 2.

A2.2 KEY FEATURES OF PART IIA

The definition of contaminated land is based upon the principles of risk assessment. The guidance follows established approaches to risk assessment, including the concept of source-pathway-receptor, sometimes referred to as contaminant-pathway-target or source-pathway-target.

Part IIA relies on a risk-based approach, which acknowledges that the risks to human health and the environment presented by given levels of certain substances will vary according to the use of the land.

The concept of pollutant linkage is central to the statutory definition of contaminated land. The concept requires there to be a source of the contamination, a receptor that can be harmed and a pathway by which the receptor can be exposed to the contaminant – the contaminant-pathway-receptor linkage.

Receptors are humans, controlled waters, specified animals and vegetation, and buildings and services. Land use influences the range of potential receptors that may be exposed to contaminant sources. Within the receptor groups, some individual receptors will be more sensitive than others. For example, children are often identified as the key category within the human receptor group, because their relative size and play habits render them more sensitive than adults and more likely to be exposed to contaminant sources.

Where land is being used for housing, for example, children are likely to be the most important human sub-group when risks to receptors are being assessed for acceptability and the need for remedial action. For other receptors, such as controlled waters that may be exposed to contaminants, site-specific factors can may affect the receptor's level of exposure in varying ways. For example, at one site the underlying geology may help protect groundwater as the receptor by breaking the pathway, whereas differing conditions at an otherwise similar site may create a pollutant linkage and present a need for action.

Key to implementing the legislation is the technical basis for identifying whether land is contaminated or not. The definition of contaminated land requires the need to resolve:

- what sort of harm is to be regarded as significant
- whether the possibility of significant harm being caused is significant
- whether pollution of controlled waters is being, or is likely to be, caused.

If any of these tests is confirmed, then the risks are viewed as unacceptable.

A substantial body of technical guidance is being produced by the Department for Environment, Food and Rural Affairs (DEFRA, formerly DETR), and the regulators on its behalf, for example the Environment Agency and the Scottish Environment Protection Agency (SEPA).

Much of this guidance has been focused on answering the questions raised by the bullets on the preceding page, namely:

- whether or not harm is significant
- whether the possibility of significant harm is indeed significant
- whether pollution of controlled waters is being, or is likely to be, caused.

In addition to the guidance that helps resolve these issues, complementary guidance has been, and is being, produced. This assists those who may either have the problem or be involved in regulating the situation.

A2.3 SECTION 161 AND WORKS NOTICES UNDER THE WATER RESOURCES ACT 1991 – KEY FEATURES

Under Section 161 of the Water Resources Act 1991, the Environment Agency has wide powers to incur expense in preventing pollution of controlled waters and in cleaning up and carrying out remedial or restorative works. The costs incurred can be recovered from the person who caused or knowingly permitted the pollution or substances to enter or threaten to enter controlled waters. The latter includes land from which pollution was, or could have been, caused.

Sections 161A to 161D authorise the Environment Agency to serve a works notice on a responsible party requiring them to clean up or prevent pollution of controlled waters. Failure to comply with a notice is an offence. The recipient can appeal against the notice. Procedural issues relating to works notices appear in the Anti-Pollution Works Regulations 1999, SI 1006.

Where there is an overlap between works notices and the Part IIA regime it appears that the Part IIA regime will generally be used first, unless the contamination relates solely to controlled waters and is not in or on land. See Environment Agency *Policy and guidelines on the use of anti-pollution works notices* [73]. These guidelines only apply to England and Wales.

Appendix 3 Selecting advisers

A3.1 GENERAL

A3.1.1 Access to advisers

Where a client is not experienced in engaging and/or instructing advisers with particular expertise, such as environmental consultants, assistance may be obtained from:

- recommendations from other members of the client team, eg a client's surveyor or lawyer
- professional associations and other organisations listed in Appendix 10
- directories.

The brief for advisers depends on the objectives set by the client. Developing a suitable brief may require expertise in its own right and, as with selecting consultants, clients may require assistance from other members of their team. As outlined in Chapter 3, to promote dialogue clients should ask advisers to submit an adviser's management plan in response to enquiries, setting out their planned approach. This is covered in Appendix 6.

A3.1.2 Instructing advisers

To establish the structure of the project team, clients should:

1   Identify issues:
    - that are to be dealt with by the client
    - where advice is required.
2   Invite submissions, review proposals and capabilities from prospective advisers taking into account:
    - discontinuities/overlaps
    - areas where the advisory team as a whole can be rationalised.
3   Resolve responsibilities/lead role(s) between project team members, inviting further submissions if necessary before engaging project team members.

A client with no experience in instructing advisers should seek legal advice on the terms of the contract. Contractual issues that commonly arise are:

- the extent and nature of the liability to be accepted by the adviser (and any subconsultants/ subcontractors the adviser intends to bring into the team) in the event of negligent work. This would include limits on the size of claims that can be made and the time within which claims must be lodged
- warranties and indemnities to be given in relation to the work (if any) by the adviser and/or the instructing client
- willingness to grant a third party a contractual right to rely on services at some point in the future
- level of current professional indemnity and public liability insurance. Many advisers may not be insured for contamination, because of pollution exclusion clauses, for example. Notwithstanding this, the limits of liability need to be critically examined to ensure that they are institutionally acceptable
- whether use of subconsultants and or subcontractors is permitted and whether the adviser will be contractually responsible for the standard of their work
- confidentiality of the results and use of reports, including the right to copy the report
- archiving reports and project documentation
- clients and their legal advisers should consider whether privilege can be claimed for reports.

A3.1.3 Reliance by third parties on an adviser's report

Advisers invariably owe a contractual duty of care to their client when preparing a report or carrying out other work. If a third party (eg a lender) chooses to rely on a report commissioned by someone else, that third party has no right of action in contract against the adviser unless appropriate provisions are included:

- the contractual benefit of the report is assigned to the third party (in which case the original client loses the benefit of the report)
- the adviser enters into a collateral warranty (ie a contract collateral to the main contract between the adviser and the original client) for the benefit of the third party. The warranty acknowledges that the third party is relying on the report and warrants that the work was carried out with the standard of care required under the main contract
- the adviser issues another copy of the report addressed to the third party.

If a client instructing an adviser anticipates that a third party will wish to rely on the report to be produced, the contract must include provisions to enable one or more of theses options to be exercised in the future. In some cases, the instructing client may wish to have the right to insist on collateral warranties being issued to more than one third party.

A3.2 LEGAL ADVISERS

As with other professions, clients have their favoured lawyers, and those experienced in property and development will use lawyers with different types of expertise. The client coming to development of previously developed land for the first time will find the recommendations of other trusted professionals to be valuable. However, the client should still check that the recommended individual has the requisite skills.

The legal team should have experience of planning, waste and contaminated land. In addition, property and construction expertise is required, in common with all development deals. If the client uses larger law firms, a selection of individuals should be able to provide the whole range of skills and knowledge needed. If the client has a solicitor with normal property and/or planning expertise, the client should consider adding a specialist environmental lawyer to the team to handle waste and contamination matters. It is not uncommon for specialists to act with other law firms or with the client's in-house lawyers.

Property lawyers are increasingly undertaking site history searches as a matter of course in commercial property transactions. The results may need to be discussed with consultants or specialist lawyers. Lawyers should not rely on environmental consultants to give legal advice for which they will not be insured. Funders have made clear they do not wish to be inundated with a mass of site history searches and the lawyer has to make some judgement on their relevance if acting for the funder and/or the client.

A range of expertise is likely to be called upon when dealing with previously developed sites. Potential scope of legal expertise required for previously developed land includes:

- property
- construction
- insurance
- planning
- waste
- contaminated land
- environmental taxation.

Table A3.1 outlines the various legal contributions that may be provided to projects.

Table A 3.1 *Legal contributions to projects on previously developed land*

Topic area	Contributions
Construction	Drafting protective provisions in contract documents and consultant appointments
	Incorporating environmental provisions in construction documents
	Liaising with consultants on site investigation and site history searches
Liabilities	Advising on present and future liabilities under statute and common law
Sale and transfer issues	Liaising with funders on contamination issues
Planning	Planning and planning agreements

A3.2.1 Criteria for selection

A curriculum vitae and/or details of experience should always be requested when engaging a lawyer, and a meeting to discuss the project should be arranged. For larger projects, the client may wish to ask for full presentations or "beauty parades" from prospective advisers. The Law Society has a formal panel for planning lawyers, but not all lawyers with requisite experience are members of the panel.

There is no panel for environmental lawyers, but most lawyers working in this area are members of the United Kingdom Environmental Law Association. This is a subscription-based organisation, however, not a professional body and it includes non-lawyers as members.

A3.3 FINANCIAL/PLANNING/INSURANCE ADVISERS

A3.3.1 Criteria for selection

The selection process for advisers should mirror that of other advisers, such as environmental consultants. The criteria for selection of environmental consultants (see Section A3.4.1) apply equally to financial and planning advisers.

- *financial advisers*. A financial adviser could be a chartered surveyor, lawyer, bank manager or an independent financial adviser falling under the rules and regulations of the Pensions Investment Authority (PIA) and the Financial Services Authority (FSA)
- *specialist insurance brokers*. Some brokers are skilled in placing specialist environmental insurance on the market
- *planning advisers*. Planning advisers may be RTPI-qualified and/or chartered surveyors
- *environmental surveyors*. Now known as chartered environmental surveyors, they are accredited by the RICS to advise on environmental issues that affect property transactions and other matters.

Legal expertise likely to be called upon when dealing with previously developed sites includes:

- planning experience with type of property that is being developed and the planning context
- environmental surveying expertise in the form of a chartered environmental surveyor
- financial awareness of the purpose to which the funding is being put and its source
- tax advice relating to potential qualifications for tax relief
- insurance as specialist insurance brokers in construction, environmental and development matters.

Table A3.2 outlines the planning, financial and insurance contributions that may be required on projects.

Table A3.2   *Planning/financial/insurance contributions to projects on previously developed land*

Topic area	Contributions
Planning	Negotiation of planning issues to planning consent giving the scale of the project in its planning context
Environmental surveying	Support skills for site acquisition
	Collation of land quality statements
	Expertise of previously developed sites that may or may not be contaminated
Financial	Raising property finance for similar projects in size, scope and location
	Negotiations relating to possible qualification for tax relief
Insurance	Nature and extent of risk exposure

A3.4   TECHNICAL ADVISERS

Recent research in *Releasing brownfields* [4] highlighted the importance of clients gaining access to expert advice and site project management skills.

There are many hundreds of companies and individuals offering consultancy services in the UK covering environmental, building and engineering matters. In some cases the choice could be influenced by the requirements of other individuals and groups who may be involved, eg a lender, a local planning authority, or the other party in a potential transaction. Any such requirements should, therefore, be ascertained before a consultant is chosen.

It may be that an adviser is engaged for the initial stages of the project but, as the development proceeds to completion, their competencies do not encompass the full range of skills required. Clients need to ensure that when advisers are engaged for earlier project stages, all information and related interpretations should be able to be used by other advisers who may be employed subsequently.

A3.4.1 Criteria for selection

A quality approach to environmental consultancy [71] recommends the factors to consider when selecting environmental consultants. The factors are also relevant to the selection of all technical advisers. Key criteria upon which clients may base selection of technical advisers are set out below:

- experience and reputation in carrying out work, eg previous projects, similar sites and developments
- capability and resources to carry out the work and complete it within the time available
- competency in health and safety in respect of the proposed scheme
- intentions to supplement resources, eg use of external subconsultants/subcontractors
- experience within multidisciplinary teams (subject to planned project team structure, their background either as lead consultant or as support consultant)
- experience/skills in communication, particularly with third parties or non-technical stakeholders
- adequacy/relevance of professional indemnity insurance and public liability insurance
- policy on conformity with relevant codes of practice
- commitments to quality management, in particular external accreditation
- commitment to continuing professional development of staff
- contractual terms and conditions for the work
- the adviser's office location with respect to location of the site
- membership of trade associations.

A3.4.2 Establishing technical expertise within the project team

The range of skills and expertise that could be required in a development project embraces many environmental and engineering issues that contribute to the construction process of buildings and infrastructure.

The list below covers the possible scope of qualified expertise that may have to be called upon to resource a project fully. However, as outlined in Chapter 3, advisers need not necessarily have to call upon every specialism. The nature of many previously developed sites will be such that a full range of specialist skills is not required. In addition, professional advisers can also obtain assistance through the high-level good practice guidance that has been commissioned at national level by policy-makers and the regulators in related fields.

Much of this guidance is applicable to a wide range of situations, but there will be "operating limits", and advisers need to be aware of the circumstances when it is not appropriate. This may be particularly pertinent when changes in site conditions are encountered that were not anticipated and that fall outside the scope of the current advisory team.

In initial enquiries, clients should, therefore, establish with prospective advisers the range of qualified specialist advice that is available. When specific qualified resources are excluded, advisers should be willing to confirm that either:

- good practice specialist guidance is available, which:
  - offers access to the specialist elements that are needed
  - is relevant to the conditions of the site in question

and

- should conditions be encountered that are outside good practice guidance criteria, advisers have made provision to act, eg either through access to relevant experts or through due notification to the client that further support is required.

The potential scope of technical expertise required for previously developed land includes:

- topographical surveying
- geotechnical engineering
- highways engineering
- infrastructure drainage engineering
- structural engineering
- services infrastructure – decommissioning/diversions
- services infrastructure – new installations
- health and safety in construction
- occupational hygiene
- geology
- hydrogeology
- hydrology
- ecology
- archaeology
- soils chemistry
- water chemistry
- toxicology
- gas/vapour contamination
- radiological contamination
- ordnance contamination

- remedial technology selection and implementation
- waste science
- waste management
- materials science – engineering/durability
- materials science – reuse/recycling.

The extent of technical experience and awareness that may have to be employed on development projects on previously developed land is shown in Table A3.3.

The findings of research into the key concerns of developers contained in *Releasing brownfields*[4] were summarised in Chapter 2. Technical issues that were considered to be particularly important to the successful completion of a scheme are highlighted by asterisks in the table below.

Table A3.3   *Technical contributions to projects on previously developed land*

Topic area	Area of contribution
Site investigation: **Geoenvironmental/Geotechnical**	
Quality control of the process	**Management and control of quality of the investigation process
Establishing historical land use data	**Establishing appropriate and relevant background data on potential site conditions
Identifying previous remediation data	**Establishing previous remediation provisions and implications for sites and neighbouring land
Risk assessment: **Geoenvironmental**	
Human health risks	Establish potential risks to, amongst others, occupiers, users, workers and trespassers of land
Risks to water environment	**Establishing risks to the water environment eg groundwater/surface water
Risks to ecology	Establishing potential risks to plants/animal life
Risks to buildings/services	Establishing risks to materials e.g. potential for deterioration or failure of a component and/or overall structure or services
Remediation: **Evaluation of remediation**	**Interpretative advice on: <ul><li>remediation criteria</li><li>sustainability issues of remediation options</li><li>scope of work</li><li>costs</li><li>programming</li><li>monitoring requirements</li></ul>

Topic area	Area of contribution

Remediation
Implementation of remediation
	**Experience in project management of remediation on previously developed sites
	
	**Support services for:
	
	   ■ design, specification of remediation strategy (including interactions with site development)
	
	   ■ geotechnical issues
	
	   ■ demolition processes
	
	   ■ implementation of remediation
	
	   ■ managing environmental protection
	
	   ■ managing health and safety issues
	
	   ■ managing planning consultation/ permissions
	
	   ■ coordinating permits/licences/controls
	
	   ■ waste management issues

Site development
 	
Scheme project management
 	
Scheme phasing and cost analysis
 	
Development programming
	**Experience in project management of development of previously developed sites
	
	**Interactions between remediation and development including implications of policy, legislation, grants/insurance (see Interactions/Awareness below)
	
	**Managing overall scheme programming for schemes. For example:
	
	   ■ investigation
	
	   ■ design
	
	   ■ demolition
	
	   ■ implementation of remediation
	
	   ■ final development

Environmental impact	Managing interactions with scheme development
Environmental protection	Managing protective measures
Development site access issues	**Resolving implications of site location on access requirements

Development infrastructure	**Managing implications of site conditions on:
	
	   ■ live/abandoned services
	
	   ■ new services

Materials specifications	Managing durability/protective measures in design/ construction

Topic area	Area of contribution
Materials recycling/reuse	Managing materials reuse and/or recycling
Ecology	Managing interactions with development
Archaeology	Managing interactions with development
Heritage	Managing interactions with development
Party wall issues	Managing interactions with neighbouring owners
Records/documentation	**Managing quality of records
Archiving	**Managing archiving processes
Interactions with other disciplines	
Policy	Awareness of implications and applicability of Government policies with previously developed land
Legal issues	Awareness of applicability of statutes and common law which relate to the subject site(s) and its locality, ie England and Wales, Scotland, Northern Ireland
Grants/allowances	Awareness of availability/processes: ■ to access grants/allowances ■ for tax relief ■ for landfill tax exemption
Site insurance	Awareness of options for site-specific insurance

Appendix 4 Selecting contractors

A4.1 SERVICES BY CONTRACTORS

Contractors can be required for any of the following services on previously developed sites.

► investigations:
  ▪ geotechnical
  ▪ services location and identification
  ▪ geoenvironmental for land and/or buildings
  ▪ soils:
    • water
    • gas
    • ordnance surveys
    • radiological surveys
    • materials identification and testing
    • asbestos/lead
  ▪ laboratory analysis
► materials management:
  ▪ materials removal from site/buildings:
    • asbestos/lead
    • ordnance
  ▪ specific waste management (removal) operations
► demolition/decommissioning:
  ▪ site obstructions
  ▪ buildings
  ▪ structures
  ▪ services
► site remediation:
  ▪ principal contractor
  ▪ specialist process technologies
► development/building/infrastructure construction
► site monitoring.

A4.2 CRITERIA FOR SELECTION

A4.2.1 Pre-qualification enquiries to contractors

Valuable feedback into contractors' competencies can be obtained through a pre-qualification process. Irrespective of the specific contractual roles, eg investigation, demolition, remediation and development, the drivers to establish contractor's capability will have similarity with criteria used in the selection of advisers.

Increasingly, there is a need for competence and expertise in handling potential environmental risks. Where time permits, face-to-face interviews, discussion and questioning may be the best way to ascertain depth of experience and understanding. Pivotal discussions should be confirmed in writing or by minute.

Key topics are listed below.

- experience and reputation:
  - what experience has the contractor had of other projects involving brownfield sites and to what extent are such projects similar to the current proposal?
  - were such projects successful and completed on time and within budget?
  - are references available from the employer on such projects?
  - what environmental issues arose on those projects and was the contractor responsible for them or did this responsibility fall to the employer or other contractor?

- capability:
  - policy for utilising in-house/subcontracting resources

- environmental/health and safety offences:
  - has the contractor or any company within the same group been prosecuted or formally cautioned for any environmental or health and safety offences in the last five years? (While it is difficult to check the answer to this enquiry, companies will be cautious in misleading employers as cases are increasingly reported in the technical press)

- health and safety competency – policy and management provisions

- environmental policy and management systems:
  - does the contractor have an environmental policy and an internal environmental management system that is independently accredited? (The health and safety policy should be reviewed at the same time.) The presence of such systems for the contractor's own business indicates a conscientious approach to environmental issues)

- environmental management plans:
  - can the contractor provide examples of plans that have been prepared for other projects and some indication of their successful implementation?
  - are the constraints imposed by, for example, waste management licensing and discharges consents and abstraction licences understood?

- current licences and certifications

- affiliations to trade bodies and standards setting bodies/institutions

- links to national accreditation schemes:
  - for laboratories, there are several accreditation schemes that provide independent certification that they have demonstrated competence in achieving its defined performance criteria for analytical activities
  - the UKAS scheme is one such example, providing accreditation for laboratories in meeting certain quality assurance and quality control requirements. This scheme is relates to individual analytical methods and there is a need, therefore, to ensure certificates are relevant to the various tests required

- adequacy of insurance

- experience in communications/notifications with other parties

- quality management policy and management provisions.

Appendix 5 The client's management plan

A5.1 INTRODUCTION

The client's management plan, outlined in Chapter 3, provides a point where project criteria and information can be brought together.

The concept of the management plan is also described in DEFRA's *Model procedures for the management of contaminated land* (see Chapter 2) to help provide a focused approach to the implementation phases of contaminated land remediation.

Suggested headings are set out in Table A5.1, but the specific composition of the management plan will be a matter for each client to determine on a project-by-project basis. Whether the plan is developed and employed as an informal *aide memoire*, or whether it is a rigorous, controlled document within a formal quality management system, it is dependent upon a client's internal management structure. Whichever approach is adopted, the recommended headings aim to direct attention to the key drivers and issues affecting development of previously developed land. This enables the management plan to act not only as an initial reference, but also as a working support document to the process.

Clients may prepare initial drafting of the management plan as a precursor to engaging advisers. Further refinement and development of the plan on to a working project document can be undertaken either by clients or external advisers.

The headings and reminders incorporated into the client's management plan are also reflected in the template contained in the *Model procedures* [16]. Accordingly, should contamination be encountered, clients should find that there will be many common aspects of the good practice approaches encouraged by the *Model procedures* that are addressed in the client's management plan.

Table A5.1   *Headings of the client's management plan*

Section	Topic area	Potential contents/consideration
1	**Development strategy**	
1.1	Overview	Use of site
		Future implications:
		■ further development plans
		Plans for site disposal
		Establishing site viability
1.2	Financial	Is a satisfactory return demonstrated?
		Is the cashflow sustainable during the cycle of development?
		Can sufficient resources be released for the acquisition of the site?
1.3	Legal	Avoiding potential regulatory action
1.4	Technical	Time scales for completion
		Design life of project
2	**Opportunities**	
2.1		Tax exemptions
		Grant funding
		Tax allowances
2.2	Technical	Potential for gaining added value through incorporation of components into comprehensive project appraisal (CPA) categories

Section	Topic area	Potential contents/consideration
3	**Screening criteria**	
3.1	Ownership	Policy on ownership issues that, if encountered, would tend to result in client declining to take further interest:
		■ is the land capable of being acquired for the scheme?
		■ are existing landowners' aspirations for value sustainable?
		■ what is the tenure – freehold or long leasehold?
		■ does the developer need to partner with the LA to use compulsory purchase order powers?
		■ does the title restrict the proposed use?
		■ is there a geared ground rent? How much?
		■ is the landlord's consent required; if so for what and when?
3.2	Value	Policy on land value issues that, if encountered, would tend to result in client declining to take further interest:
		■ has the initial appraisal analysis demonstrated sufficient robustness
		■ can external events – locally, regionally, or internationally – affect the return?
		■ is the property consultant or agent prepared to stand by the market appraisal?
3.3	Market	Policy on market-related issues that, if encountered, would tend to result in client declining to take further interest:
		■ is there a market for the property when it is completed?
		■ is there a need to obtain commitments before construction begins?
3.4	Technical	Particular site characteristics that a client views as unacceptable. Possible examples:
		■ specific forms of current and historic site use
		■ particular geological characteristics
		■ local hydrogeology/hydrology
		■ complications, eg local groundwater abstraction
		■ services and infrastructure conflicts
		■ site access ownership conflicts/costs (eg off-site works)
		■ remediation options
		■ certain remediation solutions may be viewed as unacceptable, eg difficulty in verifying completion of works to the satisfaction of key third parties/ stakeholders
		■ conflicts in remediation and development programming, eg dovetailing possible long-term monitoring commitments with site disposal
		■ waste management implications that may affect site marketability
		■ future restrictions/constraints imposed on future site management, eg limits on building/site extensions
4	**Acquisition strategy**	
		Identification and risk management of potential liabilities and quantification of financial risk
5	**Risk management options**	
5.1	Mechanisms	Available technical/financial and legal options and development exit strategies

Section	Topic area	Potential contents/consideration
5	**Risk management options**	
5.1	Mechanisms	Available technical/financial and legal options and development exit strategies
6	**Commissioning advisers**	
6.1	Requirements for advice	Procedures to identify skill requirements within project team ■ see Appendix 3 for menu of capabilities to resource projects on previously developed land
6.2	Selection and appointment	Key criteria for selection: ■ see Appendix 3
7	**Commissioning contractors**	
7.1	Selection, procurement, management policy	Key criteria for selection: ■ see Appendix 4
8	**Project organisation – project team**	
8.1	Client team	Client team composition ■ contractual arrangements for engagement ■ management/supervision of project design ■ management/supervision of construction ■ management/supervision of verification activities ■ management of continuing site involvement
8.2	Management structure/ responsibility	Project structure and roles/responsibilities
9	**Project organisation – consultations**	
9.1	Consultations	Provisions for consultations
9.2	Permits	Range and scope
	Licences	■ see Table A7.1
	Approvals	
10	**Project organisation: implementation**	
10.1	End-use construction	End-use details
10.2	Future site management issues	Related intentions for involvement on site/otherwise and implications on possible site management (eg monitoring) obligations
10.3	Public relations policy	Communication/notices/complaints
10.4	Remediation strategy	Planned remediation methods and remediation verification strategy
10.5	Construction management	Supervision and management provisions
10.6	Cost plan/cashflow	Baseline estimates/budgets and reporting/monitoring protocols
10.7	Health and safety	Requirements for incident reporting and management measures
10.8	Environmental management	Requirements for incident reporting and management measures

Appendix 5

Section	Topic area	Potential contents/consideration
10.9	Scheme programme	Key stages for progress/reporting
		Decision reviews:
		■ key milestones/dates/project reviews
		Meetings:
		■ pre-start/progress
		Project stages:
		■ phasing/completion/lead-in dates
		Procurement of advisers:
		■ invitation
		■ appointment
		Consultations:
		■ statutory groups
		■ community/topic interest groups
		Scheduling of reports:
		■ draft/final
		Third-party applications/approvals
		Financial applications:
		■ grant funding
		■ tax exemptions
		■ landfill tax
		Appointment of contractors:
		■ tender documents
		■ tender invitation
		■ appointment of contractors
10.1	Contingency planning	Pre-planning provisions to take account of and cater for implications of unexpected occurrences
11	**Records/archiving**	
11.1	Documents: archiving	Collating records and arrangements for archiving

Appendix 6 The adviser's management plan

Table A6.1 lists the range of headings that may be included in an adviser's management plan

Table A6.1   *Headings of the adviser's management plan*

Section	Topic area	Potential contents/considerations
1	**Appreciation of the brief**	
1.1	Understanding of the brief	Confirmation of terms of reference within the client's brief
1.2	Available capability	Confirmation of capability to address the client's brief and issues contained within the client's management plan
2	**Project team**	
2.1	Roles	Understanding of respective roles of the project team members
3	**Approach**	
3.1	Work planning	Appreciation and interpretation of client's brief
		Adoption of good and best practice:
		■ departures from good and best practice and justification
		Project review stages/review of continuing capability
		Means of internal/external communications
3.2	Resourcing	Project team structure:
		■ roles and responsibilities
		■ nominated personnel
		■ subconsultants
3.3	Programme	Project milestones:
		■ project reporting
		■ project review
3.4	Limitations	Caveats to be taken into account
3.5	Confidentiality	Consultations/negotiations
		Subsequent publicity
4	**Appointment**	
4.1	Appointment terms	Conditions of appointment
		Provision of warranties
4.2	Fees	Invoicing
		Fee profile

In the course of negotiations over appointments, advisers should be prepared to demonstrate their specific capability and credentials to undertake the commission for which they may be invited to apply. The adviser's management plan offers an expression of the drivers and parameters surrounding the clients' area of activity and acts as a counterpart to the client's management plan. It:

- provides the initial response to client's invitation and brief
- acts as a developing working project reference on the planned conduct of the adviser's work.

This book has outlined elsewhere the potential for anticipated conditions on previously developed sites to vary as information comes to hand. This may affect an adviser's continuing ability to provide the range of services appropriate to the scope of their commissions.

It may be that a particular issue comes to light that is outside the adviser's experience. In the case of a technical adviser, for example, specific contaminants may be discovered on the site that require specialist approaches. The management plan framework reminds the adviser where a departure from conditions and experience should be explicitly addressed.

As with the client's management plan, precisely how the adviser's management plan is employed will be a matter for clients to decide.

Appendix 7 Third-party approvals

CLR 12: *A quality approach for contaminated land consultancy* [71] summarises potential approvals that may be required for contaminated land. Table A7.1 tabulates the range of third-party approvals applicable to previously developed land.

Table A7.1   *Third-party approvals in the development of previously developed land*

Party	Permit licence application	Initial interest/ acquisition	Planning	Design ground – investigation	Design – demolition	Design – remediation	Design – development	Procurement – demolition	Procurement – remediation	Procurement – development	Implementation – demolition	Implementation – remediation	Implementation – development	Completion of dev't objectives
	Chapter in *Client's guide*	4	5	6				7						8
Landowner/occupier	Entry to site	✓		✓	✓	✓	✓					✓	✓	
	Access: site/adj land													✓
	Permits to work			✓								✓	✓	✓
	Private services			✓								✓	✓	✓
	■ auth to work													
	Party Wall Act													
	■ preliminary stage					✓	✓							
	■ application				✓							✓	✓	
Utilities	Services													
	■ clearances and/or authority to work:													
	■ water/gas/ telecom/ electricity/cable/ oil pipelines			✓								✓	✓	✓
LA planning	Planning permission including associated consultations	✓		✓	✓	✓	✓					✓	✓	
LA bldg control	Building Regulations						✓						✓	✓
Nature conservation	Habitats' interference	✓		✓	✓	✓								
	■ preliminary stage													
	■ application										✓	✓	✓	
Buildings conservat'n	Historic buildings	✓		✓	✓	✓						✓	✓	✓

Party	Permit licence application	Initial interest/ acquisition	Planning	Design ground – investigation	Design – demolition	Design – remediation	Design – development	Procurement – demolition	Procurement – remediation	Procurement – development	Implementation – demolition	Implementation – remediation	Implementation – development	Completion of dev't objectives
Chaper in *Client's guide*		**4**	**5**	**6**				**7**						**8**
Environmental regulators	Sensitive aquifers – operations over			✓	✓							✓		
	Waste mgt licences													
	■ preliminary stage		✓		✓	✓	✓							
	■ application		✓									✓	✓	
	Abstraction licence													
	■ preliminary stage		✓			✓								
	■ application											✓		
	Mobile plant licence													
	■ preliminary stage		✓			✓	✓							
	■ application											✓	✓	
	Discharge consents to:													
	■ controlled waters		✓	✓		✓	✓					✓	✓	✓
	■ sewer		✓	✓		✓	✓					✓	✓	✓
	Waste removal													
	■ Duty of care/ transfer notes			✓							✓	✓	✓	
	■ waste consignment notes			✓							✓	✓	✓	
	■ waste carrier/ broker registration			✓							✓	✓	✓	
Health and Safety Executive	Asbestos removal													
	■ survey/risk assessment			✓										
	■ preliminary stage				✓	✓	✓							
	■ application										✓	✓	✓	
	Lead removal													
	■ survey			✓										
	■ preliminary stage				✓	✓	✓							
	■ application										✓	✓	✓	
Health and Safety Executive	CDM Regulations													
	■ Form F10(Rev)		✓		✓	✓	✓	✓						
	■ appoint planning supervisor		✓	✓	✓	✓	✓							
	■ appoint principal contractor							✓						
	■ client approval of construction phase health and safety plan			✓	✓	✓	✓	✓			✓	✓	✓	

Appendix 8 Financial issues

A8.1 PARTNERSHIP SUPPORT FOR LAND AND PROPERTY REGENERATION SCHEMES

The following abstract is the executive summary of the DTLR/RICS draft guidance note: *Brownfield Improvement Grant (BIG) Partnership support for land and property regeneration schemes: direct development, speculative development, non-speculative (bespoke) development* [26], dated November 2001, describing the objectives and procedures for evaluation of developers' applications. This applies only in England.

Similar provisions in accordance with EC rules apply in Northern Ireland, Wales and Scotland.

Following the EC ruling on the Partnership Investment Programme (PIP), the government submitted revised proposals on a scheme of public-sector support for property development. The European Commission has approved these. The three schemes of most interest to developers cover:

- gap-funding for speculative development
- gap-funding for bespoke development (ie where the end-user is known)
- direct development.

Gap-funding for speculative and bespoke development work on similar rules, save for one major difference. In speculative development, the developer is considered to be the beneficiary of the grant, whereas in bespoke schemes it is the occupier. This is important because the grant is now limited according to the status of the beneficiary and the location of the scheme (see below).

Under both gap-funding schemes, like the former Partnership Investment Programme (PIP) programme, grant is limited to the minimum amount necessary to enable the development to go ahead.

Regional development agencies (RDAs) (and English Partnerships) can also assist with preparatory studies and give small-scale short-term loans. They may enter into joint ventures without restriction, provided risk and reward are shared proportionately and the developer is selected through open competition.

An independent chartered surveyor appointed by, or from, the RDA, will appraise all applications for grant, certifying all market values and verifying any costs that are not the result of competitive tenders.

Appraisers will look hard at anything more than a nominal sum for site acquisition and will not allow grant to be used to inflate land values. Where the development is for occupation by the developer or an associated company, developer's profit will not be allowed as a cost.

Grant may be paid on completion of a project or pro-rata against construction costs. If paid as the project proceeds, the appraiser will deduct savings in interest charges from the developer's finance costs.

If the development is sold within a year of completion, grant will be subject to clawback based on the sale price. If not sold after a year, clawback will be based on a valuation by an independent surveyor, and grant will be subject to further clawback if the development is sold within the following four years.

A8.2 ILLUSTRATIVE EXAMPLES – TAX RELIEF FOR REMEDIATION OF CONTAMINATED LAND

The following notes are illustrative examples of tax relief calculations relating to the remediation of contaminated land.

The detailed provisions for claiming tax relief are set out in the Finance Act 2001. Companies can claim the relief in relation to expenditure that they have incurred after 12 May 2001. There are three principal criteria that must be satisfied to be eligible for a valid claim:

- land in the UK must be acquired for the purpose of the trade carried out by the company
- at the same time as the acquisition, all or part of the land must be in a contaminated state
- the company must incur capital expenditure which amounts to a "qualifying land remediation expenditure".

In calculating the corporation tax bill of a company, any "qualifying land remediation expenditure" can be treated as an amount equal to 150 per cent of the total expenditure and this will be allowed as a deduction in computing the profits of the company for the accounting period in which the expenditure was made.

If, however, the land in question is in a contaminated state as a result of anything done or omitted to be done at any time by the company or a person with a relevant connection to the company, then any expenditure to remediate such land will not be deductible. This is to ensure that a company cannot claim tax relief for cleaning up its own contamination. A company can also be excluded from claiming by failing to act.

To be "qualifying land remediation expenditure", it must be expenditure on land which is in a contaminated state and be for the purpose of preventing or reducing the harmful effects of the contamination.

It is recognised that not all expenditure on the remediation of contaminated land will relate to its contaminated state. For example, the full extent of general site preparation and excavations are not likely to qualify, as they would have been necessary regardless of the contamination. However, provided that the company can demonstrate that the works carried out are "mainly for the purpose of cleaning up the site", the expenditure qualifies.

The types of expenditure that qualify are:

- employee costs (including salaries, national insurance and pension contributions), where such employees are directly and actively engaged in the remediation of the land. This does not include employees providing secretarial and administrative services to the company
- expenditure on materials associated with remediation
- any subcontractors involved in the remediation.

The expenditure by the company must not be subsidised in any way nor may it be met directly or indirectly by any party opther than the company. If, for example, a purchaser of land has secured an indemnity from the seller to cover remedial costs, the purchaser will not be able to claim tax relief for any expenditure that may be reimbursed.

Should a company be making a loss in any given accounting period, there are provisions in the Act that enable it to claim a land remediation tax credit.

A8.3 WORKED EXAMPLES OF TAX RELIEF FOR REMEDIATION OF CONTAMINATED LAND

	£'000	£'000
1 Scenario without the relief		
UK tax-paying company		
Proceeds		**10 000**
Land cost	1000	
Remediation	2000	
Development	5000	
Total costs		**8000**
Profit before tax		**2000**
Tax at 30 per cent		600
Profit after tax		**1400**
Return on cost		17.5%
2 Scenario with the relief		
UK tax-paying company		
Remediation expenditure incurred on or after 11 May 2001 (all rules satisfied)		
Proceeds		**10 000**
Land cost	1000	
Remediation	2000	
Development	5000	
Total costs		**8000**
Profit before tax		**2000**
Tax adjustment		
Profit before tax	2000	
Remediation costs @ 50 per cent	1000	
Profit for tax purposes	1000	
Tax at 30 per cent		300
Profit after tax		**1700**
Return on cost		21.3%
Non-tax-payer		
Proceeds		**10 000**
Land cost	1000	
Remediation	2000	
Development	5000	
Total costs		**8000**
Profit		**2000**
Return on cost		25.0%

Appendix 9 Insurance – environmental risks that can be covered during the development cycle

It is very important to consider the client's position at the various stages of risk during the development cycle and the ways in which specialist insurance can respond.

The following issues are summary notes of the risks that can be covered by insurance. Single policies are, however, available in the insurance market to cover all the development stages.

A9.1 DEVELOPMENT PHASES

Figure A9.1 below illustrates the various stages of risk.

Site acquisition			Policy expires Renewal considered
Third-party cover during site preparation phase including demolition and activities leading up to remediation	i) Third-party cover during remediation phase ii) Clean-up cost cap/cost overrun	Third-party cover during construction phase	Third-party and own-site remediation cover during policy period

Policy period – subject to insurer. Refer to specialist insurance brokers.

Figure A9.1   *The various stages of risk*

A9.1.1 Site preparation phase

Subject to receipt of adequate site investigation information, insurance is available to cover the client's legal liability arising during the site preparation phase following acquisition. Cover can include risks associated with demolition and site clearance. Where contamination is identified on site, insurers may be prepared to cover third-party risks during this phase.

A9.1.2 Remediation phase

Subject to the insurer's approval of the remediation strategy, insurance is available to cover the client's liability arising out of the remediation contract. Exposure is frequently heightened where remediation activities can cause contamination to migrate off site. It should be noted that some insurers do not provide such cost-cap cover unless the project cost exceeds a stipulated amount. This should be checked.

One of the major exposures to clients is the additional unexpected costs of cleaning up the site. Even though specific site remediation costs are estimated with a contingency for reasonable overrun included, there is a real danger that costs can exceed initial estimates and vast unforeseen clean-up costs may be incurred, leaving the balance sheet dangerously exposed and the client facing a huge loss on the project. Subject to the insurer's approval of the remediation strategy and review of the fully priced contract provided by the remediation contractor, clean-up cost-cap or cost-overrun cover will be available to the client to ensure that the costs of remediation do not exceed agreed limits. Cover is also available for additional costs to amend the remediation strategy, should this be required by the regulator.

A9.1.3 Construction phase

Subject to the provision of relevant details of the construction contract, cover is available to protect the client's liability arising from the construction activities. Construction techniques such as piling and dynamic compaction can significantly enhance risk exposure. There is also potential to create a pathway for contamination once the services are installed.

A9.1.4 Post-construction phase

From practical completion, a long-term insurance policy covering an extensive range of risks as detailed below in A9.2.

A9.2 RISKS THAT CAN BE COVERED

Policies are available with the following cover options:

A9.2.1 Third-party liability

This covers third-party liability for bodily injury and property damage and off-site remediation costs arising from sudden and/or gradual pollution from incidents occurring after the policy starts. General liability policies also cover some liabilities arising from sudden and accidental pollution.

A9.2.2 Own-site remediation

This covers the cost of cleaning up contamination on site from an incident that occurs after the policy begins.

A9.2.3 Business interruption/loss of profit

Interruption of business arising out of third-party or own-site remediation claims are covered. Cover can include loss of income, rent and continuing operating expenses.

A9.2.4 Legal defence costs

While not involving a separate policy, legal defence costs incurred in defending actions, including claims for third-party liability and own-site remediation may be covered within policies.

A9.2.5 Property transfer

This covers legal liability arising from pre-existing contamination and, generally, warranties and indemnities in contracts for mergers and acquisitions. A specialist insurance broker should be consulted to design solutions to suit clients' requirements.

A9.2.6 Combined third-party and own-site remediation

Most policies can cover all risks as described above within one policy, but third-party and own-site remediation can be purchased separately. Depending upon the insurer, these policies can be extended to include:

- stigma – diminution in value if sustained as a result of a claims for third-party or own-site remediation costs
- liabilities assumed under contract, eg warranties or deeds of indemnity
- third-party or own-site remediation costs arising out of the actions of tenants
- changes in legislation during the policy period (most policies automatically provide this cover).

A9.2.7 Clean-up cost cap/cost overrun

Cover for remediation costs that exceed an estimate and an excess agreed with the insurer can be provided.

A9.2.8 Limits of indemnity

Cover is available for amounts in excess of £100 million, although customarily much lower levels such as £1 million, £2 million, £5 million or £20 million are applied.

A9.2.9 Deductible/retentions

All policies carry a self-insured retention. These tend to vary between £25 000 and £50 000 for each and every claim, but they are negotiable. A deductible for business interruption cover is a time period, usually one month, but negotiable.

A9.3 WASTE MANAGEMENT LICENCES – SATISFYING FINANCIAL PROVISION

Clients developing on or near former landfill sites may be required to apply for waste management licences (to be known in future as PPC permits). Holders of such licences will have to make "financial provision" adequate to discharge their obligations arising from the licence. This can result in large sums being tied up for many years. An Environment Agency insurance/bonding mechanism that acts as an alternative to escrows or bank bonds is available to satisfy financial provision.

A9.4 MOBILE PLANT LICENCES – SATISFYING FINANCIAL PROVISION

In-situ and *ex-situ* techniques for remediation of contaminated land are becoming increasingly popular. The Environment Agency uses the waste licensing regime to license the remediation process rather than the site itself and the appropriate contractor is required to apply for a waste management licence with the associated "financial provision" obligations.

An Environment Agency approved pollution liability policy that acts as an alternative to escrows or bank bonds is available to satisfy financial provision under a mobile plant licence.

Clients may purchase this cover on behalf of their contractors.

Appendix 10   Contacts

A10.1 GOOD PRACTICE GUIDANCE

This section provides contacts for sources of UK guidance that are referenced in good practice documents. Names of some of the original sources have changed since publication of the relevant documents, while other sources have been incorporated within other bodies. Names of successor bodies are provided.

A10.1.1 Policy-makers and regulators

Department of the Environment, Transport and the Regions (formerly Department of the Environment)
Functions are now split between:

- Department for the Environment, Food and Rural Affairs   www.defra.gov.uk
- Department for Transport, Local Government and the Regions   www.dtlr.gov.uk
- Department for Trade and Industry   www.dti.gov.uk

Scottish Office – now:
- Scottish Executive   www.scotland.gov.uk

Welsh Office – now:
- Welsh Assembly   www.wales.gov.uk

Department of Environment (Northern Ireland)   www.doeni.gov.uk

English Heritage   www.english-heritage.org.uk

Environment and Heritage Service in Northern Ireland   www.ehsni.gov.uk

Environment Agency   www.environment-agency.gov.uk

HM Customs and Excise   www.hmce.gov.uk

Scottish Environment Protection Agency   www.sepa.gov.uk

Scotland and Northern Ireland Forum for Environmental Research (SNIFFER)   See Scottish Environment Protection Agency

Welsh Historic Monuments Executive Agency (CADW)   www.cadw.wales.gov.uk

Health and Safety Executive   www.hse.gov.uk

Highways Agency   www.highways.gov.uk

Historic Scotland   www.historic-scotland.gov.uk

Parliamentary Office of Science and Technology   www.dti.gov.uk/ost

A10.1.2 Research organisations/professional bodies/trade and sectoral representative bodies/standards setting bodies

Association of Geotechnical and Geoenvironmental Specialists   www.ags.org.uk

British Bankers Association   www.bba.org.uk

British Drilling Association   www.britishdrillingassociation.co.uk

British Geological Survey   www.bgs.ac.uk

British Standards Institution   www.bsi-global.com

British Urban Regeneration Association   www.bura.org.uk

Building Research Establishment	www.bre.co.uk
Chemical Industries Association	www.cia.org.uk
Construction Industry Research and Information Association	www.ciria.org.uk
Confederation of British Industry	www.cbi.org.uk
English Heritage	www.english-heritage.org.uk
English Nature	www.english-nature.org.uk
exSite Research Ltd	www.exsite.org
Friends of the Earth	www.foe.co.uk
House Builders Federation	www.hbf.co.uk
Institute of Field Archaeologists	www.archaeologists.net
Institute of Petroleum	www.petroleum.co.uk
Institution of Chemical Engineers	www.ichem.org
Institution of Civil Engineers	www.icenet.org
Institute of Environmental Health Officers	www.cieh.org.uk
International Standards Organisation	www.iso.ch
Loss Prevention Council	www.bre.co.uk/lpc/index.html
National Housing Federation	www.housing.org.uk
National House Builders Council	www.nhbc.co.uk
Royal Institution of Chartered Surveyors	www.rics.org
Scottish Enterprise	www.scottish-enterprise.com
Transport Research Laboratory	www.trl.co.uk
UKAS	www.ukas.com
United Kingdom Environmental Law Association	www.ukela.org
Water Research Centre	www.wrcplc.co.uk
Welsh Development Agency	www.wda.co.uk

A10.2 DEVELOPMENT AGENCIES IN THE UK AND REGIONAL DEVELOPMENT AGENCIES

A10.2.1 English Partnerships

English Partnerships was created in its current form in May 1999 by combining the Commission for the New Towns (CNT) with the national functions of the Urban Regeneration Agency (URA – previously known as English Partnerships).

The aim of English Partnerships is to promote the regeneration of areas of need through the reclamation, development or redevelopment of land and buildings, with due regard to statutory guidance issued by the secretary of state.

English Partnerships' published vision for its role is "the national force for regeneration and development working in partnership to create new jobs and investment through sustainable economic regeneration and development in the English regions" and "the national catalyst for property-led regeneration". The emphasis is on the national role and property skills. Its aim is to:

- create quality places to live and work
- increase the resources available for regeneration
- help the government meet its target of accommodating at least 60 per cent of new household growth on previously developed land.

A10.2.2 Regional development agencies

Regional development agencies (RDAs) cover eight English regions, together with London, They aim to co-ordinate regional economic development and regeneration, enable the English regions to improve their relative competitiveness and reduce the imbalances that exist within and between regions.

RDAs have the following statutory purposes:

- to further economic development and regeneration
- to promote business efficiency, investment and competitiveness
- to promote employment
- to enhance development and application of skill relevant to employment
- to contribute to sustainable development.

Their specific functions are:

- to formulate a regional strategy in relation to their purposes
- regional regeneration
- to take forward the government's competitiveness agenda in the regions
- to take the lead on regional inward investment
- to develop a regional skills action plan to ensure that skills training matches the needs of the labour market
- take a leading role on European funding.

A10.2.3 Welsh Development Agency

Established by the UK Government in 1976, the Welsh Development Agency has subsequently grown to encompass a wide range of functions related to economic development and regeneration. Since 1999, the Agency has been sponsored by the National Assembly for Wales. It operates throughout Wales, working with businesses, local authorities and communities to achieve the objective of "sustaining the best business climate in Europe by facilitating the growth of quality jobs and competitive industry for the benefit of people throughout Wales".

The principal mechanisms by which this is pursued are

- business support and advice to industry
- attraction of inward investment from around the world.

In addition, the Agency assists industry through the development of industrial and commercial property and the assembly of land for new development.

Improvement and protection of the environment, urban regeneration and community regeneration are key functions that underpin the business objectives and enhance the quality of life for all residents. The Agency has a remit to support the delivery of the National Assembly's sustainable development agenda and to work with all partners in the pursuit of design quality in all new development.

A10.2.4 Scottish Enterprise

Scottish Enterprise is Scotland's main economic development agency, funded by the Scottish Executive. Its mission is to help the people and businesses of Scotland succeed and to build a world-class economy. Key priorities are to:

- help new businesses get under way
- support and develop existing businesses
- help people gain the knowledge and skills they will need for tomorrow's jobs
- help Scottish businesses develop a strong presence in the global economy – building on Scotland's reputation as a great place to live, work and do business.

A10.3 CONTACT ADDRESSES – REGENERATION

The following organisations are involved in regeneration:

English Partnerships

Arpley House, 110 Birchwood Boulevard, Birchwood, Warrington, Cheshire WA3 7QH

Tel: 01925 651144

Welsh Development Agency

Principality House, The Friary, Cardiff CF10 3FE

Tel: 0845 777 5577

Scottish Enterprise

150 Broomielaw, Atlantic Quay, Glasgow G2 8LU

Tel: 0141 248 2700

Regional Development Agencies

Advantage West Midlands, 3 Priestley Wharf, Holt Street, Birmingham B7 4BN

Tel: 0121 380 3500

East of England Development Agency

The Business Centre, Station Road, Histon, Cambridge CB4 9LQ

Tel: 01223 713900

East Midlands Development Agency

Apex Court, City Link, Nottingham NG2 4LA

Tel: 01159 888300

London Development Agency

Devon House, 58–60 St Katherine's Way, London E1W 1JX

Tel: 020 7680 2000

North West Development Agency

PO Box 37, King's Court, Scotland Road, Warrington,WA1 2FR

Tel: 01925 400100

One North East

Great North House, Sandyford Road, Newcastle Upon Tyne NE1 8ND

Tel: 0191 261 2000

South East England Development Agency

Berkley House, Cross Lanes, Guildford GU1 1YA

Tel: 01483 484200

South West of England Regional Development Agency

Sterling House, Dix's Field, Exeter, Devon EX1 1QA

Tel: 01392 214747

Yorkshire Forward

Victoria House, 2 Victoria Place, Leeds LS11 5AE

Tel: 01133 949600

A10.4 CONTACT ADDRESSES – INFORMATION RELATING TO PROFESSIONAL ADVISERS

Association of Consulting Engineers

Alliance House, 12 Caxton Street, Westminster, London SW1H 0QL

Tel: 020 7222 6557

Association of Consulting Scientists Limited

PO Box 560, Wembley, Middlesex HA0 1NN

Tel: 020 8991 4883

Association of Geotechnical and Geoenvironmental Specialists (AGS)

39 Upper Elmers End Road, Beckenham, Kent BR3 3QY

Tel: 020 8658 8212

British Consultants Bureau (BCB)

1 Westminster Palace Gardens, 1–7 Artillery Row, London SW1P 1RJ

Tel: 020 7222 3651

British Geotechnical Society

c/o Institution of Civil Engineers, 1 Great George Street, Westminster, London SW1P 3AA

Tel: 020 7222 7722

British Geological Survey (BGS)

Sir Kingsley Dunham Centre, Keyworth, Nottingham NG12 5GG

Tel: 0115 936 3100

Chartered Institute of Environmental Health (CIEH)

Chadwick House, Rushworth Street, London SE1 0QT

Tel: 020 7928 6006

Chartered Institution of Water and Environmental Management (CIWEM)

15 John Street, London WC1N 2EB

Tel: 020 7831 3110

English Nature

Northminster House, Peterborough, PE1 1UA

Tel: 01733 455 000

Environmental Consultants Group (ECG)

Environmental Industries Commission, 6 Donaldson Road, London NW6 6NB

Tel: 020 7624 2728

Geological Society

Burlington House, Piccadilly, London W1V 0JU

Tel: 020 7434 9944

Institute of Environmental Management and Assessment (IEMA)

Welton House, Limekiln Way, Lincoln LN2 4US

Tel: 01522 540069

Institution of Civil Engineers

1 Great George Street, Westminster, London SW1P 3AA

Tel: 020 7222 7722

Institution of Structural Engineers

11 Upper Belgrave Street, London SW1X 8BH

Tel: 020 7235 4535

Landscape Institute

6/7 Barnard Mews, London SW11 1QU

Tel: 020 7738 9166

Law Society

113 Chancery Lane, London WC2A 1PL

Tel: 020 7242 1222

Royal Institution of Chartered Surveyors

12 Great George Street, Parliament Square, London SW1P 3AD

Tel: 020 7222 7000

Royal Institute of British Architects

66 Portland Place, London W1N 4AD

Tel: 020 7307 3677

Royal Society of Chemistry (RSC)

Burlington House, Piccadilly, London W1V 0BN

Tel: 020 7437 9107

Royal Town Planning Institute (RTPI)

26 Portland Place, London W1N 4BE

Tel: 020 7636 9107

UKELA

General Secretary, Dr Christina B T Hill, Honeycroft House, Pangbourne Road, Upper Basildon, Berks RG8 8LP

Tel/Fax: 014 9167 1631

A10.5 WEBSITES FOR OTHER ORGANISATIONS

Inland Revenue:

List of disadvantaged areas   www.inlandrevenue.gov.uk/so/disadvantaged.htm

Appendix 11   Data management

A11.1 SITE LOGS

The development of a site log is highlighted in Chapter 3 as a key component of data management. Examples of documents to be included within the site log are:

- documents appointing advisers

- the main contract documents and any documents referred to in them and any undertakings given between lawyers

- title documents or copies including leases and wayleave agreements

- legal enquiries and searches obtained on site acquisition and details of public register entries

- funding documentation: both banking documents and grant applications and agreements

- the planning permission and environmental impact assessment and any letters varying those or dealing with approval of detailed design or changes; planning policy documents and any development brief or interim policy documents relating to the site; Section 106 planning agreements and highways agreements

- the construction contract documents and tender documents including related specifications and bills

- any separate works agreements with utilities or third parties

- duty of care transfer notes and special waste consignment notes and documentation dealing with landfill tax and landfill tax exemptions

- waste management licences, discharge consents and abstraction licences and trade effluent consents or agreements

- insurance policies and certificates: these may be site-specific or be copies of group cover held. There may also be site-specific environmental policies

- site investigation reports: it is essential that originals of the final versions of all site reports are available. Any collateral warranties and duty of care deeds related to such reports should be included if available to the client

- CDM documentation: copies of the health and safety plan and file should be available

- as-built drawings and drawings of services and utilities

- press releases and published documents and cuttings relating to the site.

A11.2 LAND QUALITY STATEMENTS

The Royal Institution of Charted Surveyors guidance note *Contamination and its implications for chartered surveyors* [25] has provided for a land quality statement that deals with the commercial implications and real estate issues arising from the development or acquisition of brownfield or contaminated assets.

In addition to the information provided by the land condition record, the land quality statement would include six questions that are germane to most property transactions. These questions were devised in the unpublished CIRIA guidance note *Guidance on the sale and transfer of land which may be affected by contamination* [67] and need to be assessed at every phase of the development life cycle:

i.   Is remedial treatment necessary or prudent to enable continued use of the property for its current use without undue risk to the health of persons using the property? If so, how much would this treatment cost? Is this a fair measure of an appropriate reduction in value?

ii.   Is remedial treatment necessary or prudent to reduce the risk of damage to a third party's health or property, or damage to the environment that may give rise to a claim for damages, prosecution or action by the appropriate regulatory bodies? If so, how much would this treatment cost? Is this a fair measure of an appropriate reduction in value?

iii.   If remedial treatment is not warranted under i or ii above, but there remains a residual risk of future claims from third parties and regulatory authorities, what reduction in value (if any) is appropriate to compensate for this risk?

iv.   Does concern regarding the risks associated with the known or suspected presence of contamination restrict the prudent use of the properties as compared to the likely range of possible uses if the site was uncontaminated? What reduction in value (if any) should there be to reflect this? Can this restriction be reasonably measured by the cost of remedial treatment to overcome the restriction on the use of the property?

v.   If the property were to be redeveloped, how much additional expense would be incurred in investigating contamination of the property further and carrying out any necessary remedial work as compared to an uncontaminated property? What reduction in value (if any) is appropriate to reflect this fact?

vi.   If the property is being treated for contamination, what reduction in value (if any) is appropriate to compensate the purchaser for the fact that the property was once contaminated or for the possibility that the treatment, despite appearances, has not been successful? Or alternatively, would the site increase in value if it can be demonstrated that the land is absolutely free of risk in this respect?

A11.3 SITE REPORTS

Table A11.1 below summarises the possible range of reports that may be developed as part of the development process on previously developed land.

Table A11.1   *Reports for previously developed sites*

Chapter	Stage in *Client's guide*	Report/typical contents
4	Initial appraisal	Client report:
		▪ Financial modelling/project viability
		▪ Liability issues
		▪ Buildability
		▪ Geotechnical
		▪ Geoenvironmental:
		• contamination
		• archaeology
		• ecology
		• noise
		• air quality
		▪ Infrastructure:
		• access
		• services
		▪ Other sustainability issues
		▪ Waste
		Health and safety file
		Site log

Chapter	Stage in *Client's guide*	Report/typical contents
5	Planning	Environmental assessment
6	Detailed design	Site investigation: ■ factual data ■ interpretative risk assessment Demolition/remediation: ■ strategy ■ detailed design ■ cost estimates Site development: ■ method statements ■ detailed design ■ cost estimates Health and safety file Site log
7	**Construction phase:** **Procurement** Demolition/remediation	Tender evaluation Project cost review/estimation Site log
	Site development	Tender evaluation Project cost review/estimation Site log
	Implementation: Demolition/remediation	Contract progress: ■ programme/cost ■ waste management applications/working plans/records ■ environmental management/protection ■ inspections – regulators/other third parties ■ health and safety ■ as-built information ■ scheme verification Health and safety file Site log
	Site development	Contract progress: ■ programme/cost ■ waste management applications/working plans/records ■ environmental management/protection

Chapter	Stage in *Client's guide*	Report/typical contents
		■ Inspections – regulators/other third parties
		■ Health and safety
		■ As-built information
		■ Scheme verification
		Health and safety file
8	Completion of the development objectives	
		Site monitoring records
		Site log
		Health and safety file
		Land condition records
		Land quality statements

Appendix 12   Documents relevant to policy in Scotland, Wales and Northern Ireland

The following documents have relevance to previously developed land in Scotland, Wales and Northern Ireland respectively. Refer to Chapter 5 for a summary of planning issues.

A12.1 SCOTLAND

Policy

Scottish Executive Circular 1/2000. *Environmental Protection Act 1990: Part IIA Contaminated land.* Available from the Scottish Executive.

Framework for local authority – SEPA liaison under Part IIA of the Environmental Protection Act. Available from SEPA website.

Legislation

Contaminated Land (Scotland) Regulations 2000, SI No 178

National Planning Policy Guidelines (NPPGs)

NPPG 1	*The planning system*
NPPG 2	*Business and industry*
NPPG 3	*Land for housing*
NPPG 4	*Land for mineral working*
NPPG 5	*Archaeology and planning*
NPPG 7	*Planning and flooding*
NPPG 10	*Planning and waste management*
NPPG 11	*Sport and physical recreation and open space*

Planning Advice Notes

PAN 33	*Development of contaminated land*
PAN 36	*Siting of new housing in the countryside*
PAN 37	*Structure of planning*
PAN 38	*Structure plans housing and land requirements*
PAN 40	*Development control*
PAN 42	*Archaeology – the planning process and scheduled monument procedures*
PAN 44	*Fitting new housing into the landscape*
PAN 50	*Controlling the environmental effects of surface mineral workings*
PAN 51	*Planning and environmental protection*
PAN 52	*Planning and small towns*
PAN 56	*Planning and noise*
PAN 57	*Transport and planning*
PAN 58	*Environmental impact assessment*
PAN 59	*Improving town centres*
PAN 60	*Planning for natural heritage*
PAN 61	*Planning and sustainable urban drainage systems*
PAN 63	*Waste management planning*

A12.2 WALES

Legislation

Contaminated Land (Wales) Regulations 2001, WSI No 2197

Technical advice notes

TAN 1	*Joint housing land availability studies*
TAN 4	*Retailing and town centres*
TAN 5	*Nature conservation and planning*
TAN 11	*Noise*
TAN 12	*Design*
TAN 15	*Development and flood risk*
TAN 21	*Waste*

A12.3 NORTHERN IRELAND

Planning policy

PPS 1	*General planning principles*
PPS 2	*Planning and nature conservation*
PPS 3	*Development control: roads considerations*
PPS 4	*Industrial development*
PPS 5	*Retaining and town centres*
PPS 6	*Planning, archaeology and built heritage*
PPS 7	*Quality residential developments*
PPS 9	*The enforcement of planning control*

Issued for consultation

PPS 8	*Open space, sport recreation leisure and community facilities – issues*
PPS 11	*Planning and waste management*

Development control advice notes

08	*Small unit housing in residential areas*
10	*Environmental impact assessment* (revised)
12	*Hazardous substances* (2nd edition)

Development Control Advice Notes

In addition to the Planning Policy information and the Development Control Advice Notes, the Department of the Environment in Northern Ireland issues development plans relating to districts in Northern Ireland.

Further information is available on the website: www.doeni.gov.uk.

Appendix 13   Solicitor's warning card

This appendix reproduces the full text of the Law Society's *Warning card to solicitors* issued in 2001 [28]. Reference can also be made to an article in the *Law Society's Gazette* of 29 November 2001, "Contaminated land regime – warning to all" [75]. A more detailed version of this paper can be found on the UKELA website: www.ukela.org.uk.

Warning ~ To All Solicitors ~ Contaminated Land Liabilities

The advice contained on this Card is not intended to be a professional requirement for solicitors. Solicitors should be aware of the requirements of Part IIA of the Environmental Protection Act 1990 but they themselves cannot provide their clients with conclusive answers. They must exercise their professional judgement to determine the applicability of this advice to each matter in which they are involved and, where necessary, they should suggest to the client obtaining specialist advice. In the view of the Law Society the advice contained in this Card conforms to current best practice.

Solicitors should be aware that environmental liabilities may arise and consider what further enquiries and specialist assistance the client should be advised to obtain.

Contaminated Land

1. The contaminated land regime was brought into effect in England on 1 April 2000. It applies to all land, whether residential, commercial, industrial or agricultural. It can affect owners, occupiers, developers, and lenders. The legislation, which is contained in Part IIA, Environmental Protection Act 1990 and in regulations and statutory guidance issued under it* is retrospective. It covers existing and future contamination.

    The National Assembly is expected shortly to introduce similar regulations regarding contaminated land in Wales.

2. Local authorities must inspect and identify seriously contaminated sites. They can issue remediation notices requiring action to remediate contamination, in the absence of a voluntary agreement to do so. In certain cases ("Special Sites") responsibility for enforcement lies with the Environment Agency.

    A negative reply to the standard local authority enquiries from the local authority may merely mean the site has not been inspected. It does not necessarily mean there is no problem.

    Compliance can be costly, and may result in expenditure which could exceed the value of the property.

    Liability falls primarily on those who "cause or knowingly permit" contamination (a Class A person). If the authority cannot identify a Class A person, liability falls on a Class B person, the current owner, or occupier of the land. Class B persons include lenders in possession. There are complex exclusion provisions for transferring liability from one party to another. Some exclusions apply only on the transfer of land, or the grant of a lease. The applicability of any relevant exclusion needs to be considered before entering such transactions.

*   See Contaminated Land (England) Regulations 2000 SI 2000/227 and DETR Guidance on Contaminated Land, April 2000,

In every transaction you must consider whether contamination is an issue.

Conveyancing transactions

In purchases, mortgages and leases, solicitors should:

1.   Advise the client of potential liabilities associated with contaminated land.

Generally clients should be advised of the possibility and consequences of acquiring interests in contaminated land and the steps that can be taken to assess the risks.

2.   Make specific enquiries of the seller.

In all commercial cases, and if contamination is considered likely to be a risk in residential cases (eg redevelopment of brownfield land).

3.   Make enquiries of statutory and regulatory bodies.

4.   Undertake independent site history investigation, eg obtaining site report from a commercial company.

In commercial cases, if there is a likelihood that the site is contaminated.

5.   Advise independent full site investigation.

6.   Consider use of contractual protections and the use of exclusion tests.

This may involve specific disclosure of known defects, possibly coupled with price reduction, requirements on seller to remedy before completion, and in complex cases the use of warranties and indemnities.

Unresolved problems, consider

7.   Advising withdrawal, and noting advice.

8.   Advising insurance (increasingly obtainable for costs of remediation of undetected contamination and any shortfall in value because of undisclosed problems).

Specific Transactions

1.   Leases

Consider if usual repair and statutory compliance clauses transfer remediation liability to tenant, and advise.

2.   Mortgages

Advise lender, if enquiries reveal potential for or existence of contamination, and seek instructions.

In enforcement cases, consider appointment of receivers, rather than steps resulting in lender becoming mortgagee in possession, and so treated as a Class B person.

3.   Share sales and asset purchases

Consider recommending the obtaining of specialist technical advice on potential liabilities, use of detailed enquiries, warranties and indemnities.

Other Relevant Legislation

Other legislation and common law liabilities (eg nuisance) may also be relevant when advising on environmental matters including:

Water Resources Act 1991

Groundwater Regulations 1998

Pollution Prevention and Control (England and Wales) Regulations 2000

Further Information

Law Society's Environmental Law Handbook (4th edition, 2001)

DETR's website: www.detr.gov.uk

Index

Please note that figures and tables are in italics.

contaminant migration, insurance against 92
contaminated land
    definition under Part IIA 117
    government objectives regarding 27
    and previously developed sites 26-8
    statutory definition 27
    suitable for use approach 27-8
    tax incentives for 20, 45
    tax relief for remediation of 138-9
    under Part IIA regime, risk transfer 46-7
    valuation of 26
Contaminated land — management of financial risk, CIRIA report 44
Contaminated Land (England) Regulations 2000 58
contaminated land liabilities, solicitor's warning card 46, 101, 157-8
contaminated land use
    current, and the Part IIA regime 27
    new land uses 28
contamination
    contamination mechanisms 26
    and the impact on financial risk 28
    remediation of a negative factor 26
    as a reserved matter in outline planning consent 63
    see also gas contamination; land contamination
Contamination and its implications for chartered surveyors RICS guidance note 42, 151-2
contract management, information for 94
contractors 127-28
    demolition contractors 73
    engagement of for site investigation 69
    pre-qualification enquiries 90, 127-28
    public liability insurance 92
    service provision 127
    setting obligations of 94
    specialist, accommodation of 94-5
    see also consultants and contractors
Control of Pollution (Amendment) Act 1989 96
Control of Substances Hazardous to Health Regulations (COSHH) 70
Controlled Waste (Registration of Carriers and Seizure of Vehicles) Regulations 1991 96
controlled waters, regulation of discharges to/abstractions from 39
Council for the Protection of Rural England (CPRE), on the thwarting of brown field initiatives 113
Countryside Council for Wales 40
CPA *see* Comprehensive Project Appraisal (CPA)
Customs and Excise 40, 88
    Landfill Tax Guidance Note 2 96

D

data management 41-2, 47, 151-4
    action points on information handling 42
    'as built' drawings 105
    developing the site log 72, 76, 81-2, 84, 97, 99
    format of records for collection and dissemination 41-2
    overview and the site log 41
    value of site log at point of sale 102
DEFRA (Department for the Environment, Food and Rural Affairs)
    Model Procedures documents 29, 49, 77, 84-5, 99
    other guidance publications 85
    policy and regulatory roles 38
demolition, good practice guidance 87
demolition contractors 73
demolition and decomissioning design, key issues 73-6
    archaeology 75
    communication/consultation with third parties 75
    consents/permits/licences 74
    embracing sustainable development criteria 75
    health and safety 74

management of environmental protection 74
    nature conservation 74
    reviewing advisers 73-4
    waste 74
Department of the Environment 51, 96
Department of the Environment Northern Ireland 38
derelict land *see* previously developed land
desk studies 47-8
    and walkover stages 66
DETR (Department of the Environment, Transport and the Regions) (2000)
    Circulars 58, 64
    Planning Policy Guidance Notes 25, 27, 56, 62, 64
developer's manual, creation of 33
development
    opportunity led 21
    pressure to use land for 17
development agencies
    contact points 145-6
    roles of 40, 145-50
    UK, and regional development agencies 146-48
development design, key issues 82-4
    archaeology 83
    communicating proposals with planners/consultees/regulators 83-4
    communication and consultation with third parties 84
    consents/permits/licences 82
    embracing sustainable development 84
    health and safety issues 82-3
    management of environmental protection 83
    nature conservation 83
    reviewing advisers 82
    waste management of environmental protection 83
    will remediation strategy integrate with development planning and design? 82
development and developers 116
development objectives, completion of 101-7
    key guidance 107
    key issues 102-7
    policy and professional issues 101
development process
    driven by combination of interactive forces 115, *115*
    interactions and overlaps *18*, 19
    key educational support tools
    see also planning process
development schemes, site-specific 76-7
development strategy, devising of 32-8
    client's management plan for previously developed land 33, *34*
    client's site acquisition strategy 34-5, *35*, 36
    supporting the business case 32-3
documentation
    creation of site log 41, 151
    design issues, incorporation into construction procurement document 92-3
    simplicity and transparency the key 57-8
DoE (Department of the Environment) 85, 87
    Planning Obligations (Circular 1/97) 58, 64
    The Use of Conditions in Planning Permissions (Circular 11/95) 58, 64
DTLR (Department for Transport, Local Government and the Regions) 38
    development of guidance on land contamination 28, 60
    Technical Advice Note, Development on land affected by contamination (draft) 59, 60
Duty of Care Transfer Notes 96

E

economic restructuring, and Brownfield development 115
English Heritage 39
English Nature, conservation and site protection 40
English Partnerships 44, 146-7
environment agencies

Model procedures for the management of contaminated land: DEFRA/Environment Agency, key technical reference texts 29, 49, 77

N

National House-Building Council (NHBC) 39, 52
nature conservation 69, 74, 79-80, 83, 94
negotiations/discussions, at pre-application stage 56-8
new households, projected growth in 17
noise/vibration 75
non-governmental organisations (NGOs) 56
    and development schemes 40

O

options to purchase 35
orphan sites, clean up of 59
Our Towns and Cities: the Future — Delivering an Urban Renaissancee, White Paper 64, 113
own site remediation insurance 142

P

Partnership Investment Programme (PIP) 137
permits *see* consents/permits/licences
planners/consultees/regulators 83, 99
    consultations and discussions to agree on remediation strategy 80
Planning: delivering a fundamental change, Green Paper 59, 60-1
planning advisers 121-2
planning application
    consultees on 38-40, 63
    formulation of 53, 61-3
    key guidance and policy documents 64
    outline or detailed 63
    scope of 62
planning authorities
    decide on planning application type 63
    detail required 59-60
    existing guidance for dealing with contaminated land 58, 145-50
    intrusive investigation requirement 59
planning conditions
    in planning permissions 58, 63
    reflected in contract obligations 93, 103
planning guidance, significant new developments 60-1
planning, key issues 55-63
    application formulation 61
    pre application 55-61
Planning Policy Guidance Notes (DETR) 64
    Note 3 *Housing* (DETR) 25, 27, 56
    Note 9 Nature Conservation 62
planning process *54*, 55
    interactions with stages of development 53, *54*
    planning authorities 38
    pre-application issues 53
planning team, development of 55
policy appraisal, pre-application 55-6
Pollution Prevention and Control (England and Wales) Regulations 2000
    permits required under 95-6
    and site investigation reports 59
potentially harmful substances, occurrence of 26
preliminary investigations 47-8
    detailed site investigation at acquisition 48
    effects of ignoring good practice 48
previously developed land
    building and development control 39
    client's management plan for 33, *34*
    defined 25
    development constrained by site acquisition 115

documents relevant to policy in Scotland, Wales and Northern Ireland 155-6
    facilitating release of in property transactions 35
    health and safety legislation applicable to projects on 70
    local concerns over insufficiently detailed remedial strategies 57
    opportunities provided by 19-21
    other key parties and their roles 39-40
    planning process 38-9
    policy and regulation 38
    scope of planning application 62
    specific issues of relevance 70
    technical contributions to projects on *124-7*
    third party approvals *135-6*
professional indemnity insurance 91-2, 104-5
Property Misdescriptions Act 1991 102
property transfer insurance 142
protected species on site, and type of assessment required 61-2
public-private joint initiatives, major waterfront development 19
public-sector investment initiative, project management with shared duties 93

Q

quality assurance and quality control 67, 127-28

R

radon gas 26
reclamation, in major waterfront development 19
redevelopment
    design guidance on 29
    preparation for 31-42
    see also previously developed land
regeneration
    contact addresses 148-9
    partnership support for 19, 19, 137
Regional Development Agencies (England) 40, 44, 137, 147
Regional Planning Guidance Notes (RPGs) 64
regulators *see* planners/consultees/regulators
regulatory consent, liaison with regulatory bodies 63
Releasing Brownfields, P.M. Syms 43
    developers and planners 57
    project management 89
remediation
    accommodating specialist contractors 94-5
    and development design, health and safety issues 82-3
    insurance cover during 141
remediation design 76-82
    archaeology 80
    communicating proposals and consulting with planners/consultees/regulators 80
    design of the remediation strategy 76-7
    embracing sustainable development 81
    extent of investigations 81
    good practice guidance 87-8
    health and safety 79
    landfill tax and landfill tax exemptions 78
    management of environmental protection 79
    nature conservation 79
    reports 80
    requirements for consents/permits/licences 78
    will the design integrate with development planning and design? 77-8
reporting structures, consistent, achievement of 49
reports 73, 152-4
    continuing communications and consultations 76
    structure/content of 41-2, 67
risk assessment(s) 81
    previously developed land 46-7

Index